Ambrose / Harris

PRINT & FINISH

v. the process of producing
printed material

v. complete the manufacture
or decoration of printed
material

An AVA Book

Published by AVA Publishing SA

Rue des Fontenailles 16, Case postale,

1000 Lausanne 6, Switzerland

Tel: +41 786 005 109 Email: enquiries@avabooks.ch

Distributed by Thames & Hudson (ex-North America)

181a High Holborn, London WC1V 7QX, United Kingdom

Tel: +44 20 7845 5000 Fax: +44 20 7845 5055

Email: sales@thameshudson.co.uk

www.thamesandhudson.com

Distributed in the USA and Canada by:

Watson-Guptill Publications

770 Broadway, New York, NY 10003

Fax: +1 646 654 5487 Email: info@watsonguptill.com

www.watsonguptill.com

English Language Support Office

AVA Publishing (UK) Ltd.

Tel: +44 1903 204 455 Email: enquiries@avabooks.co.uk

ISBN 2-940373-42-6 / 978-2-940373-42-0

10 9 8 7 6 5 4 3 2 1

Design and text by Gavin Ambrose and Paul Harris

www.gavinambrose.co.uk

Original photography by Xavier Young

www.xavieryoung.co.uk

Original series concept devised by Natalia Price-Cabrera

Production and separations by AVA Book Production Pte. Ltd., Singapore

Tel: +65 6334 8173 Fax: +65 6259 9830 Email: production@avabooks.com.sg

Print & Finish

Client: The End
Design: The Kitchen
Technical overview:
Contrast of tactile greyboard cover stock, with high reflectivity, blue foil-block illustration

The End

This is the cover of a brochure that was designed by The Kitchen for The End, a London nightclub. *The End Biography* celebrates the club's tenth anniversary and features commentary from music journalists, specially commissioned artist illustrations and a supplementary photo section. The cover features an illustration of the club's entrance by Will Barras, which is foil-blocked in blue into a greyboard stock. The fine line artwork reproduces well in the foil and provides a dramatic contrast with the raw quality of the greyboard.

Contents

Faydherbe / De Vringer

SEA Design

Turnbull Grey

Studio KA

HGV Felton

Studio Myerscough

Graphic designers have an array of print processes and finishing techniques at their disposal with which to produce eye-catching and effective publications. Printing is the process of putting ink on to a substrate, but the method a designer chooses to use to do this will depend on practical factors such as cost, volume and time, in addition to more aesthetic factors such as the quality of the visual result required. Different print processes such as letterpress, offset lithography and screen printing allow a designer to mix these variables to obtain different results, but that does not have to be the end of the printing process. Most printed products can be enhanced by some kind of finishing technique once the ink is on the paper, such as folding, die cutting, foil blocking or tipping-in coloured plates.

Substrates

Substrates come in many different weights, colours and textures and can have a dramatic impact on the end result of the job, adding texture or some other quality. This section looks at the advantages and restrictions certain stocks offer.

Printing

Different techniques for applying ink on to a substrate, such as offset lithography, screen printing, gravure and letterpress, can be used to produce creative effects, which derive from the characteristics of the processes themselves.

Finishing

Various processes can be used to provide the final touches to a print job, including die cutting, embossing, debossing, foil blocking and varnishing, which can transform an ordinary looking piece into something much more special.

Production

The physical production processes can be harnessed by the designer to produce creative results, perhaps by manipulating channels and plates or changing the order in which the process colours print so that you control the processes rather than letting them control your work.

Binding

Different binding methods such as Canadian, French folding, case and perfect, give a designer a range of different functionalities and visual qualities, which can add a special touch to a publication.

Resolve

Many printed items incorporate a range of the techniques that are discussed in this book. Interesting printing, foiling, finishing and material choices are found on the examples showcased in this section.

Client: Ministry of Health, The Netherlands
Design: Faydherbe / De Vringer
Technical overview: Embossed title for added depth and texture

Zorg Zonder Zorgen

This is the cover of *Zorg Zonder Zorgen* (Healthcare Without Worries), a brochure created by Dutch design studio Faydherbe / De Vringer. The cover features a photographic contact sheet depicting images of those people interviewed in the brochure. The title of the publication is superimposed over the contact sheet in white type, which is embossed to give it added depth.

This book introduces different aspects of printing and print finishing via dedicated chapters for each topic. Each chapter provides numerous examples of creative print and finishing techniques from leading contemporary design studios, which are annotated to explain the reasons behind each of the design choices made.

Key design principles are isolated so that the reader can see how they are applied in practice.

Clear navigation

Each chapter has a clear strapline to allow readers to quickly locate areas of interest.

Introductions

Special section introductions outline basic concepts that will be discussed.

Tipping-in and tipping-on

A tip-in refers to the attachment of a single page into a printed publication by wrapping it around the central fold of a section and gluing along the binding edge.

If a tipped-in page is shorter than the publication's pages then it needs to be aligned at either their top or bottom edge. Tipping-in to the central slither can prove problematic as there is no page edge to align it with. Fine-art prints are sometimes printed intaglio and tipped-in. Tipping-in should not be confused with inserts, which are loose, unattached items that are placed inside a publication.

Tipping-on

Tipping-on involves pasting a smaller element, such as an illustration or reply slip, on to a publication, as can be seen in the example on the facing page.

Tipped-in page with short return   **Tipped-in page, aligned top**   **Tipped-in page full-width**

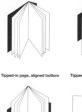

Tipped-in page, aligned bottom   **Tipped-on insert**   **Tipped-in page**

Print & Finish Substrates

Gagosian Gallery
This is *Six Paints and a Sculpture*, a book that celebrates the work of Cy Twombly. It was created by Bruce Mau Design for the Gagosian Gallery in New York. The book features tipped-on colour plates. Each of the plates was produced separately, and then applied to the book.

Intaglio
A technique that describes the printing of an image from a recessed design that is incised or etched into the surface of a plate. The ink lies recessed below the surface of the plate and transfers to the stock under pressure and stands in relief on the stock.

Client: Gagosian Gallery
Design: Bruce Mau Design
Technical overview:
Tipped-on colour plates

Print & Finish Tipping-in and tipping-on

Diagrams

Diagrams add meaning to theory by showing the basic principles in action.

Examples

Commercial projects from contemporary designers bring alive the principles under discussion.

Additional information

Clients, designers and printing and finishing technique overviews are included.

Supporting material

Additional reference material is included to add context to the examples.

Written explanations

Key points are explained within the context of an example project.

Related information

Related information, such as terminology definitions, is isolated and explained.

Print & Finish How to get the most out of this book

Client: Robert Cary-Williams
Design: Studio Thomson
Technical overview:
Litho-printed Plike and use of
printing ink that resembles
hand-drawn, chalked text

`1917`

ROBERT CARY-WILLIAMS

Spring Summer 2005

Wednesday 22nd September at 7.30 pm

BFC Tent Duke of York Square

Kings Road London SW3 4RY

RSVP

mike@concretelondon.com

Tel: 020 7434 4333

Fax: 020 7434 4555

X Name _____

X Seat _____

(studio thomson)

A substrate is any stock of material that receives a printed image, ranging from a standard sheet of paper to more elaborate and tactile papers and boards, and even extends to promotional items such as coffee mugs, t-shirts and, as we'll see, the human body.

The substrate selected for a particular print job will be determined by its ability to 'take' a printed design and the overall aims and intention of the piece of work, as the examples in this section will illustrate. For instance, excellent image reproduction in colour magazines requires a different substrate than that used for newspapers, where low cost is more of a priority. In addition to printability, substrates are often selected for the other qualities that they can lend a design such as a tactile stimulus.

Substrate selection is a vital consideration at the start of the design process. The variety of substrates to print upon is now greater than ever before, giving wider creative possibilities for designers; as colour, weights and textures all have a bearing on the effectiveness of a piece. Identity design schemes, for example, can be strengthened through consistent use of stocks, which generates an element of individuality.

Robert Cary-Williams (left)

This invitation was created by Studio Thomson for UK fashion designer Robert Cary-Williams. The design is printed on a Plike (plastic-like) paper substrate that is made from polymer resin and applied to the surface of the paper with an off-line coating machine. The dark colour of the substrate and its tactile quality combine with the printing ink to create the illusion of blackboard and chalk. For added realism, chalk was used on the mailing envelopes; giving each invite varying degrees of distress

Paper types
Paper types refers to any stock or substrate that can be printed with one of the conventional printing processes.

Paper type	Notes	Primary uses
Newsprint	Paper made primarily of mechanically ground wood pulp, shorter lifespan than other papers, cheap to produce, least expensive paper that can withstand normal printing processes.	Newspapers, comics.
Antique	Roughest finish offered on offset paper.	To add texture to publications such as annual reports.
Uncoated woodfree	Largest printing and writing paper category by capacity that includes almost all office and offset grades used for general commercial printing.	Office paper (printer and photocopy paper, stationery).
Mechanical	Produced using wood pulp, contains acidic lignins. Suitable for short-term uses as it will 'yellow' and colours will fade.	Newspapers, directories.
Art board	Uncoated board.	Cover stock.
Art	A high-quality paper with a clay filler to give a good printing surface, especially for halftones where definition and detail are important. Has high brightness and gloss.	Colour printing, magazines.
Cast coated	Coated paper with a high-gloss finish obtained while the wet coated paper is pressed or cast against a polished, hot, metal drum.	High-quality colour printing.
Chromo	A waterproof coating on a single side intended for good embossing and varnishing performance.	Labels, wrappings, and covers.
Cartridge	A thick white paper particularly used for pencil and ink drawings.	To add texture to publications such as annual reports.
Greyboard	Lined or unlined board made from waste paper.	Packaging material.

Client: Country Casuals
Design: Turnbull Grey
Technical overview:
Flock substrate used to
add tactile quality

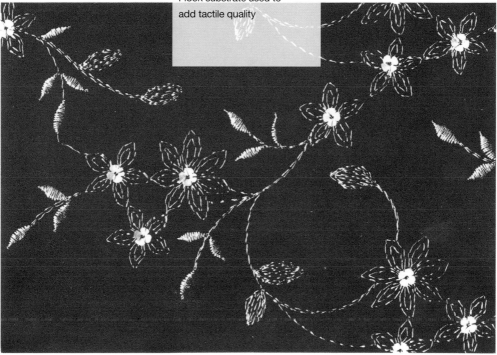

Country Casuals

This invitation to a fashion preview show was created by Turnbull Grey design studio for clothing manufacturer Country Casuals. The use of a tactile flock substrate works as a visual simile to a piece of cloth, and reinforces the nature of the event that is being publicised.

Flock

A speciality cover stock that is produced by coating a sheet with size, either entirely or partially, and then applying a dyed flock powder, which is made from very fine woollen refuse or vegetable fibre dust, to the substrate. Flock was originally intended to simulate tapestry and Italian velvet brocade. Nowadays, it is used to give a decorative, delicate and luxurious feel to designs. Flock fibres tend to be absorbent and therefore do not provide a good printing surface for conventional offset lithography, but more viscous inks can be used without any problem. The relatively robust nature of a flocked substrate means it can be used with both embossing and foil-blocking.

Client: Lucky Voice
Design: MadeThought
Technical overview:
Design embossed into gold
Astrolux mirror board

Lucky Voice

This is an invitation to private karaoke venue, *Lucky Voice*, which was created by MadeThought design studio. The design is embossed into gold Astrolux, a highly reflective mirror board. Although the design is simple, the way in which it harnesses the qualities inherent in the substrate is quite exquisite.

Astrolux
Astrolux is a highly reflective, high-gloss card that is available in a wide range of colours.

The George Hotel & Brasserie

These menu cards were created for The George Hotel & Brasserie by Gavin Ambrose. The design is printed on to an uncoated stock so that the menu cards can be overprinted with each day's menu options using the hotel's printing equipment. This solution meets the hotel's practical requirements to offer a different daily menu by printing the cards on demand, and also allows the hotel to present its guests with a professional menu presentation that conveys the assured daily freshness of its food. The uncoated stock is slightly textured and this serves to soften the cards' images.

Client: The George Hotel & Brasserie
Design: Gavin Ambrose
Technical overview: Uncoated stock for overprinting on demand

Overprinting

A technique where one element of a design is printed over another to add texture and/or modify the colours or content of a design.

Client: Squire and Partners
Design: Thomas Manss
& Company
Technical overview:
Particle-board substrate and
finishing touches to reflect
architecture

Squire and Partners (above)

This corporate brochure for London architectural firm Squire and Partners was
created by Thomas Manss & Company. Rather than presenting the work in a typical
corporate document, which inevitably has a limited shelf life, the designers opted
for a more lavish presentation of the firm's architectural designs and projects.
The particle-board cover carries a simple foil stamp, reflecting the firm's trademark
clean, modern lines and attention to detail. The cover has a monolithic appearance,
reminiscent a block of carved stone, adding a degree of permanence and quality.

d-raw Associates (right)

This business card was created for interior designers d-raw Associates by
MadeThought design studio. It features silver-foil type that has been stamped
into light coloured greyboard, which results in a minimalist, subtle, tone-on-tone
effect. The coarse fibres of the stock contrast with the accuracy afforded by the
foil-stamp process.

Print & Finish Substrates

Client: d-raw
Design: MadeThought
Technical overview:
Silver-foil stamp into greyboard
for minimalist effect

Client: University of the
Arts, London
Design: Turnbull Grey
Technical overview:
Translucent cover and
duplicated design creates
moiré effect

UNIVERSITY OF THE ARTS
LONDON

Inauguration Ceremony
Banqueting House
Whitehall
London

11 May 2004

Client: RIBA

Design: Studio Myerscough

Technical overview:
Translucent stock printing
magenta and black

Annie Spink Award Brochure (above)

This is a brochure for the Annie Spink Award for Excellence in Education, which is awarded by the Royal Institute of British Architects. The brochure was created by Studio Myerscough and is printed in magenta and black on a translucent stock, and the text is reproduced as a surprint. The overall impact is subtle, refined and inviting. The brochure also features French fold pages with stitch-sewn binding.

University of the Arts, London (left)

This is the programme for an inauguration ceremony for the University of the Arts, London, which was created by Turnbull Grey design studio. The programme's cover is printed on to a translucent substrate that allows the reader to see the paper stock underneath. The paper stock carries the same design as the cover, but is reproduced in blue with white lettering. The combination of the two produces a moiré effect on the typography.

Print & Finish Paper types

Client: Stadscollective
Den Haag
Design:
Faydherbe / De Vringer
Technical overview:
Varied stocks and print
techniques

A Decade of Difference

This is a series of cover designs created by Faydherbe / De Vringer for a collection of books by Stadscollective Den Haag that were presented as gifts to special visitors to The Hague. Eight different artists were invited to contribute to the books. To provide a degree of uniformity, Faydherbe / De Vringer created collages, using different typefaces, of numerals for each cover in the series. The numerals were printed in two spot colours, which were specifically selected to contrast with the colours of each of the eight paper stocks. Covers 6 and 8 are embossed; covers 2, 4 and 5 overprint; covers 1 and 3 are printed in metallic silver and cover 7 knocked out.

Unusual substrates

Virtually any material can be used as a substrate to receive a design, although each presents its own application challenges.

Substrate	Uses	Application process
Metal	Signage, objects or report covers.	Screen print, transfer, hand-painted/drawn, die cut.
Ceramic	Objects.	Ceramic, hand-painted/drawn.
PVC	Signage, report covers or objects.	Screen print, die cut, transfer.
Fabric	Clothing, banners or report covers.	Screen print, hand-painted/drawn.
Human body	Promotional events.	Hand-painted/drawn, transfers.
Wood	Signage or objects.	Burnt, screen print, hand-painted/drawn.

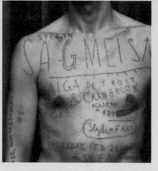

Metal

This is an invitation created by Howdy design studio for an event hosted by human resources company Boldly Go. It features the date of the event, die cut into a metal substrate, and the organisation's email address is also etched into it.

Human Body

This poster (detail) was created by New York design studio Sagmeister Inc. for AIGA Detroit. Stefan Sagmeister asked an intern to cut the poster design into his skin to convey the pain that accompanies his design projects. The result is both powerful and shocking.

Wood

This invitation, created for Her House gallery by Studio Myerscough, is silk-screen printed on to a wood substrate. The slab-serif typeface has a solid quality, which allows it to work effectively with the rough wood grain surface.

Client: Zaha Hadid
Design: Thomas Manss
& Company
Technical overview:
Moulded plastic outer
catches light, protects and
lends tactility

Print & Finish Unusual substrates

Zaha Hadid

This book sleeve was created for architectural firm Zaha Hadid by Thomas Manss &
Company. Its moulded plastic outer creates a simple, yet intriguing statement due to
the way it catches the light, and this adds value to the design. The transparent plastic
also serves to provide both a protective layer and a tactile element to the high impact
design and lends it a modernist simplicity.

Client: Staverton
Design: SEA Design
Technical overview:
Yellow perspex provides
distinctive and weighty invite

Design Prima
2005
Billingsgate

May 17–19
Stand T16

RSVP
T +44 (0)20 7731 9565
info@staverton.co.uk
www.staverton.co.uk

Staverton

Diesel (right)

This invitation was created for fashion label Diesel by George & Vera design studio. The design is screen printed on to transparent, blue-toned perspex, which results in the production of a distinctive and unusual object and is more substantial than it would have been had a paper stock been used. The use of perspex turns a disposable invite into something altogether more permanent.

Staverton (left)

This is an invitation for Staverton furniture that was created SEA Design. Using the yellow of the client's corporate identity as a building block, SEA Design screen printed white text on to blocks of yellow perspex in order to create a distinctive and weighty invitation. The result is an innovative use of material that is uniquely different from the usual use of paper stocks.

Client: Diesel
Design: George & Vera
Technical overview:
Perspex substrate is distinctive and permanent

launch

art

therese stowell

DIESEL
FOR SUCCESSFUL LIVING

Florence
www.
florencefineart.
com

Laurent-Perrier
CHAMPAGNE

Armada

Print & Finish Unusual substrates

Client: John Rocha
Design: SEA Design
Technical overview:
Silk-screen printed type on
black perspex

Cut to Black (above)

This is the press invitation to the launch of a new collection by John Rocha at
Waterford Crystal, which was created by SEA Design. Details of the event have
been silk-screen printed on to a simple piece of black perspex, which transforms
the invitation into an object that feels weighty and important.

Tapestry (right)

This announcement card was created by SEA Design to promote the 'Tapestry'
range of fabric-inspired paper stocks produced by paper merchant GF Smith.
The piece was produced on the 'Cotton White' substrate from the range, and is
embossed with a digitised broderie anglaise pattern. Text was applied as a bronze
foil stamp that still allows the floral pattern in the substrate to show through.

Broderie Anglaise
Is a style of embroidered fabric, usually white cotton, in which holes are cut in delicate patterns and oversewn.
Broderie anglaise is frequently used to embellish lingerie, shirts and skirts.

The new ~~fab~~
inspired ~~galle~~
from GFSmith

Tapes

Client: GF Smith
Design: SEA Design
Technical overview:
Board substrate with
embossed broderie
anglaise pattern, and
bronze foil-stamped text

London
GF Smith
2 Leathermarket
Weston Street
London SE1 3ET

phone
7407 6174

mile
03 1037

gfsmith.co

Print & Finish Unusual substrates

Showthrough

Showthrough occurs when ink printed on one side of a page can be seen on the other (non-printed) side; showthrough is usually determined by the type of substrate used.

Thin and absorbent stocks, with little filler or coating material, are most susceptible to showthrough. Some stocks have such a degree of transparency that subsequent pages will also showthrough. Showthrough is generally viewed as a defect, although it can be used deliberately and creatively to great effect.

Memo (above and right)

This is a periodical produced for architecture firm Magyar Marsoni. It features a transparent Vellum insert that covers the opening image. The delicate nature of the Vellum adds a tactile dimension to the publication, while allowing the opening image to showthrough the introductory text.

Client: Magyar Marsoni
Design: Untitled
Technical overview:
Vellum insert adds tactile
dimension and allows the
image to showthrough

Welcome to issue one of MEMO, a new periodical
from Magyar Marsoni Architects. There is a ready
supply of publications about architecture and of people
ready to make their views known about it. Our intention
with MEMO is not so much to publish or make news
as to generate a less heated, more reflective discussion
of current issues in architecture as they affect a practice
that is, in size at least, representative of the majority in
the UK. MEMO gets its name from its loose, informal
nature. The text is, literally, a discussion: the sort of
ad hoc, after hours dialogue that provides both solace
and inspiration to us in the midst of running an
architectural practice. Each conversation, each edition
of MEMO, will centre loosely on a theme. The first theme
is, appropriately enough, ORIGINS.

Client: Boot

Design: Untitled

Technical overview:
Lightweight bible paper
provides showthrough and
image and text interaction

When intentionally used, translucent showthrough can create a multi-layered textural effect as different elements build on top of one another.

Chris Boot Ltd

This is a catalogue created by Untitled for Chris Boot Ltd, a contemporary photography book publisher. The publication incorporates a lightweight bible paper that enables both the production of a thin book and a small amount of showthrough between pages. Images merge seamlessly with text, creating a light, textured feel.

Print & Finish Showthrough

Imposition

Imposition is the arrangement of a printed publication's pages, in the sequence and position they will appear when printed; before being cut, folded and trimmed.

An imposition plan provides a visual guide with which a designer can easily see, for example, the colour fall in a section or the arrangement of different stock choices as the imposition plan shown opposite demonstrates.

5	12	6	8
4	13	16	1

7	10	11	9
2	15	14	3

This book is printed in 16-page sections.

The flatplan (left) shows the page fall on a sheet of paper. The sheet of paper will be printed on both sides and then folded and cut to produce a 16-page section. As each side of the sheet prints on a different pass, a different special colour can be used on either side. However, the application of a special colour will only be available to those eight pages that are on the same side of the paper sheet, either pages 1, 4, 5, 8, 9, 12, 13 and 16 or pages 2, 3, 6, 7, 10, 11, 14 and 15. When folded, pages 1 and 2 (highlighted) back up.

An imposition plan serves several functions. As well as allowing the designer to easily see where different colours and stocks fall it can also show how they can be used to maximum effect. For example, if the budget allows the use of a special colour on one page, the imposition plan will show the range of pages within a section that could also use the special colour at no extra cost in order to enhance the design.

Printing pass
A pass is a term used to describe the movement of a sheet of stock through a printing press. The stock literally passes through the press.
Special colour
A special (or spot) colour is one that is specially mixed to give a precise hue.

Print & Finish Substrates

This book is printed and bound in 16-page sections. As such there are eight pages to 'view' (i.e. eight pages on each side of a single section's paper sheet).

| 1 | 2 | 3 | 4 | 5 | 6 | 7 | 8 | 9 | 10 | 11 | 12 | 13 | 14 | 15 | 16 |

Stock: Gloss art
Prints: CMYK

| 17 | 18 | 19 | 20 | 21 | 22 | 23 | 24 | 25 | 26 | 27 | 28 | 29 | 30 | 31 | 32 |

Stock: Grey-coloured stock
Prints: CMYK

| 33 | 34 | 35 | 36 | 37 | 38 | 39 | 40 | 41 | 42 | 43 | 44 | 45 | 46 | 47 | 48 |

Stock: Gloss art
Prints: CMYK

| 49 | 50 | 51 | 52 | 53 | 54 | 55 | 56 | 57 | 58 | 59 | 60 | 61 | 62 | 63 | 64 |

Stock: Buff-coloured stock
Prints: CMYK

| 65 | 66 | 67 | 68 | 69 | 70 | 71 | 72 | 73 | 74 | 75 | 76 | 77 | 78 | 79 | 80 |

Stock: Woodfree, uncoated stock
Prints: CMYK

| 81 | 82 | 83 | 84 | 85 | 86 | 87 | 88 | 89 | 90 | 91 | 92 | 93 | 94 | 95 | 96 |

Stock: Matt art
Prints: CMYK

| 97 | 98 | 99 | 100 | 101 | 102 | 103 | 104 | 105 | 106 | 107 | 108 | 109 | 110 | 111 | 112 |

Stock: Matt art
Prints: CMYK and Pantone 9101 on eight pages

| 113 | 114 | 115 | 116 | 117 | 118 | 119 | 120 | 121 | 122 | 123 | 124 | 125 | 126 | 127 | 128 |

Stock: Matt art
Prints: CMYK, Pantone 8062 and Pantone 811 on eight pages

| 129 | 130 | 131 | 132 | 133 | 134 | 135 | 136 | 137 | 138 | 139 | 140 | 141 | 142 | 143 | 144 |

Stock: Green-coloured stock
Prints: CMYK

| 145 | 146 | 147 | 148 | 149 | 150 | 151 | 152 | 153 | 154 | 155 | 156 | 157 | 158 | 159 | 160 |

Stock: Gloss art
Prints: CMYK

| 161 | 162 | 163 | 164 | 165 | 166 | 167 | 168 | 169 | 170 | 171 | 172 | 173 | 174 | 175 | 176 |

Stock: Kraft paper
Prints: Black only (K)

Print & Finish Imposition

One Tate, four galleries
Tate Modern

Housed in the former Bankside Power Station on the south bank of the Thames, Tate Modern is Britain's national museum of international modern art. Tate Modern offers differing perspectives on contemporary art with exhibitions and displays covering the full spectrum of media, including film and photography. The vast space of the Turbine Hall is used to dramatic effect for changing commissions designed to utilise the scale, atmosphere and acoustics of the building.

1,2 — Collection display
3 — Turbine Hall

20 — 21

'I feel childlike at Tate Modern. The size, the scale… I feel awed' — Member

Membership benefits
Enjoying more

Members Rooms
Members Rooms at Tate Britain and Tate Modern are exclusively for the use of Members. The Tate Modern Members Room has spectacular views across to St Paul's Cathedral and is a popular place to meet, especially on Friday and Saturday evenings and Sundays during the day.

TATE ETC. magazine
TATE ETC. magazine is sent to you three times a year in January, May and September, to coincide with seasonal changes in Tate's exhibition calendar. The magazine offers international perspectives, diverse opinions and comment on the visual arts and Tate's programme to add to your personal experiences of exhibitions and displays.

Tate guide
Members receive advance notice of the forthcoming programme at all four galleries, via the Tate guide sent every other month. The guide covers exhibitions, the latest Collection displays, and a wide range of special events. From talks by artists to films to children's workshops, the events programme offers many ways to explore and learn more about art.
The guide also provides all the contact and access details you need to plan your visit or book for events, while the Members page gives you the latest news and offers.

Membership benefits
Enjoying more

10 — 11

Print & Finish Substrates

Tate Galleries

This is the members' handbook for the UK's Tate Galleries created by NB Studio. It features colour sections that are printed on high-gloss white stock, which is spliced between sections of uncoated coloured stock. This results in a contrast between the tactile quality of the coloured stock with the high reflectivity of the laminated, white stock.

Client: Tate Galleries
Design: NB Studio
Technical overview:
Creative imposition of high-gloss, white stock spliced between coloured stock

Foreword
Welcome to Tate

Thank you for becoming a Tate Member. We value your support enormously and I hope you will enjoy this closer association with Tate and take full advantage of the benefits of membership.

Whether you visit frequently or occasionally, Members are part of Tate and play a vital role in our success. Your enthusiasm helps us to draw in and inspire new visitors, and creates energy throughout the galleries. You share our belief in the ability of art to change lives, and are invaluable advocates. The financial support you provide enables us to purchase and preserve works of art for the Collection, and to bring the visual arts to increasingly diverse audiences through Tate's innovative series of exhibitions, events and education programmes.

Museums and galleries have enormous potential to liberate the imagination, open doors to the past and reflect the creative energy of the present; with your help we hope to realise this potential. Thank you for supporting us today and playing your part in shaping the Tate of the future.

Nicholas Serota
Director

'There is something indefinable, even magical, about Tate St Ives'
— Member

One Tate, four galleries
Tate St Ives

Tate St Ives opened in 1993 to provide a focus for the St Ives School of artists within the British modern movement, while today also supporting contemporary art through the Artist in Residence scheme. The gallery has a spectacular coastal setting, with large windows and balconies offering views across Porthmeor Beach and the opportunity to appreciate the extraordinary quality of light for which St Ives is famous. Exhibitions of work by established and emerging artists are presented throughout the year, alongside changing Collection displays of painting and sculpture by artists with a connection to St Ives.

1 — View of the gallery
2 — Collection display

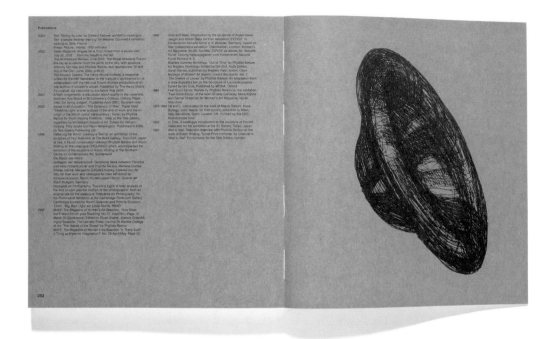

Publications

2003 Text *Tasting for Lear* for Edward Fellows' exhibition catalogue. Text a severe weather warning for Melanie Counsell's exhibition catalogue, Séte, France
Erase: Picture, Istanbul, 1952 with text

2002 *Sadé Magazine*, Angera de la Cruz: notes from a studio visit. July 22, 2002 ...from the mouth to the far.
The Architecoan Review, June 2002: The Royal Academy Forum, the city as sculpture: from the plinth to the sky, with speakers Anthony Gormley and Phyllida Barlow, and reproduced as 'In and Out of the City', June 2002, p.99-91
The Shrapnel Sparks: The Henry Moore Institute, a response written for the HMI Newsletter to the Institute's conference on its collaboration with the National Sound Archive production of an oral archive of sculptor's voices. Published by The Henry Moore Foundation. Quotations by Liz Aston. Feb 2003

2001 Artists' Assignments: a discussion about quality in the visual arts. Southern Arts Board at St Catherine's College, Oxford. Paper titled On Being Judged. Published April 2001, Southern Arts.

2000 Issues in Art Education: *The Dynamics of Now*. Paper titled 'Travelling Light: a brief analysis of the end of work and the triumph of the 35mm colour transparency'. Given by Phyllida Barlow for 'From Varying Positions', 1998, at the Tate Gallery, organised by Wimbledon School of Art. Edited by William Furlong, Polly Gould and Paul Hetherington. Published in 2000, by Tate Gallery Publishing Ltd.

1998 *Retracing the World*: Catalogue Text for an exhibition of the sculpture of Paul Matisuhm, at The INAX Gallery, Tokyo104, Japan at Sea. A Faxed conversation between Phyllida Barlow and Alison Wilding for the catalogue GROUNDED which accompanied the exhibition of the sculpture of Alison Wilding at the Northern Centre for Contemporary Art, Sunderland
Die Macht des Alters
Strategien der Meisterschaft. Telephone Texts between Christine and Irene Hohenbühler and Phyllida Barlow, Marlene Dumas, Elfriede Jelinek, Margareta Schütte-Lihotzky, Lidewien van de Ven, for their work and catalogue for their exhibition at Nonprivatopians, Berlin. Kunstmuseum Bonn, Galerie der Stadt Stuttgart, Germany.
Postcards on Photography, 'Travelling Light' A brief analysis of the end of work and the triumph of the photographic: from an original talk for the catalogue 'Postcards on Photography' for the Photorealist exhibition at the Cambridge Darkroom Gallery, Cambridge (curated by Naomi Salaman and Ronnie Simpson. 'Girth', 'Big, Bad, Ugly' ed Linda Moore. NBAD

1997 *MAKE: The Magazine of Women's Art* Section, 'How Does the P Meet Inform your Teaching' No.77, Sept/Nov, Page 19
Make 3D Conference. Edited by Stuart Evans, Joanna Greenhill. Ingrid Swenson. The Lethaby Press, Central St Martins College of Art. 'The Hatred of the Object' by Phyllida Barlow
MAKE: The Magazine of Women's Art Section 'Is There Such a Thing as Material Imagination?' No. 15 April/May, Page 22

1996 *Hide and Seek*, Introduction to the sculpture of Ander Heral Jaeger and Alison Gaira for their exhibition 'SYZYGY' to Fordowverein Aktuelle Kunst e. V, Munster, Germany, issued on their collaborative exhibition 'Clandestine', London. Women's Art Magazine No.59, Apr/May. SYZYGY as above, for 'Aktuelle Kunst' Zeitung herausgegeben vom Fordevverein Aktuelle Kunst Munster e. V.
Brajdes Summer Workshop, 'Out of Time', by Phyllida Barlow for Brajdes Workshop. Edited by Gill Ord, Andy Cohen, Sarah Davies, published by Brajdes Park, Ipston, Oxon
Museum of Modern Art pitponi. *Louise Bourgeois*, Vol. 1
The Sweine of Louise by Phyllida Barlow. An sculpture from a slide illustrated talk on the Sculpture of Louise Bourgeois. Edited by Ian Cole. Published by MOMA, Oxford

1995 *Feel Good Factor*, Review by Phyllida Barlow for the exhibition 'Feel Good Factor' of the work of Leila Galloway, Mira Kojima and Rachel Chapman for Women's Art Magazine, No.64 May/June

1993-1994 '95 and I', Introduction to the work of Marco Bettori, Rosa Buttajj, John Isaacs, for their touring exhibition in Milan, Italy. Barcelona, Spain. London, UK. Funded by the EEC Kaleidoscope fund.

1992 *In Time*. A catalogue introduction to the sculpture of Hiroshi Watanabe for his exhibition at the Art Gallery, Tokyo, Japan.

1992 *Wall to Wall*. Television interview with Phyllida Barlow on the work of Alison Wilding. Turner Prize nominee, for Channel 4. 'Wall to Wall' Productions, for the Tate Gallery, London.

252

Pyramid
Scaffolding, varnish, skating, plywood, dye, timber lengths. 600 x 150 x 800 cm 1997
Margate Design Centre, London

At Sea: a conversation by fax between Phyllida Barlow and Alison Wilding 22.08.98 – 02.09.98

Bible Paper

Also called India paper, this is a thin, strong and lightweight paper. Bible paper is opaque and, as its name suggests, is often used in the production of bibles and other books with a large number of pages.

Phyllida Barlow

This brochure about the work of sculptor Phyllida Barlow, was created by Gavin Ambrose for Black Dog Publishing. Barlow uses low-tech materials in her work including those she finds in scrap yards. A variety of paper stocks help define different sections of the publication and add texture to it. The brochure uses kraft stock, coated stock, uncoated stock and bible paper.

Client: Black Dog Publishing

Design: Gavin Ambrose

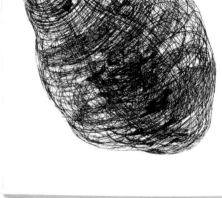

Phyllida Barlow's
Sculptural
Imagination
Mark Godfrey

Technical overview:
Imposition of a variety of
paper stocks to add texture

The Sneeze
of Louise
Phyllida Barlow

Bunk#
27 plywood boxes
Each 30 × 30 × 30 cm
1969

This essay is adapted from a slide-illustrated lecture on the sculpture of Louise Bourgeois and refers to work seen during 1995 in the exhibitions *Rites of Passage* at the Tate Gallery Millbank, London, *Louise Bourgeois* at the Musee d'Art Moderne de la Ville de Paris, and *Louise Bourgeois: Sculpture* and *The Prints of Louise Bourgeois* at the Museum of Modern Art, Oxford. The slide illustrated talk emphasised a narrative interpretation of the sculpture as well as identifying the rich formal concerns inherent to the work. The working title for the talk was 'Telling Tales: interpreting Louise Bourgeois' sculptural narratives.

Whilst looking at Louise Bourgeois' *Cells* and *The Red Rooms* in the Musee de l'Art Moderne de la Ville de Paris and the Tate Gallery, London I thought about the devices artists have used during this century to frame and contain disparate things so as to bring unlikely, opposing or contrasting objects together as a unified experience - devices such as boxes, plinths, cages and, of course recently, the ubiquitous vitrine.

I recalled Marcel Duchamp's *Why Not Sneeze, Rrose Selavy* of 1921. As a small, neat object it is easy to remember. Its disparate collection of things are unified by a small, portable cage. The ring on top is just big enough for a finger to go through suggesting a container for the lightest of animals - small birds to be transported to and from market. It is therefore a portable object which, as such, clearly shows the signs of wear and tear.

It contains a collection of white cubes, apparently trapped. Though marble is a dense, heavy material the cubes masquerade perfectly as cubes of sugar. Protruding into the cubes are two objects: a thermometer and a cuttle bone. The thermometer is an instrument which measures and records the changes in body temperature, registering sickness or health, but here, as it nestles and probes into the cool deceitful cubes of marble sugar, what change is expected to be detected? Perhaps a rise in temperature would cause an explosion and the

168

169

Tipping-in and tipping-on
A tip-in refers to the attachment of a single page into a printed publication by wrapping it around the central fold of a section and gluing along the binding edge.

If a tipped-in page is shorter than the publication's pages then it needs to be aligned at either their top or bottom edge. Tipping-in to the central slither can prove problematic as there is no page edge to align it with. Fine-art prints are sometimes printed intaglio and tipped-in. Tipping-in should not be confused with inserts, which are loose, unattached items that are placed inside a publication.

Tipping-on

Tipping-on involves pasting a smaller element, such as an illustration or reply slip, on to a publication, as can be seen in the example on the facing page.

Tipped-in page with short return

Tipped-in page, aligned top

Tipped-in page full-width

Tipped-in page, aligned bottom

Tipped-on insert

Tipped-in page

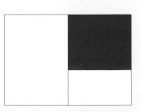

Gagosian Gallery

This is *Six Paints and a Sculpture*, a book that celebrates the work of Cy Twombly. It was created by Bruce Mau Design for the Gagosian Gallery in New York. The book features tipped-on colour plates. Each of the plates was produced separately, and then applied to the book.

Client: Gagosian Gallery
Design: Bruce Mau Design
Technical overview:
Tipped-on colour plates

Intaglio

A technique that describes the printing of an image from a recessed design that is incised or etched into the surface of a plate. The ink lies recessed below the surface of the plate and transfers to the stock under pressure and stands in relief on the stock.

Client: Autograph ABP
Design: Untitled
Technical overview:
Gloss, colour pages tipped-in
to black stock

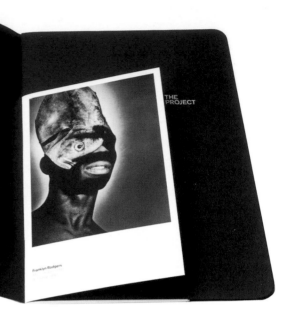

THE
PROJECT

Franklyn Rodgers

Cover illustration
© 2003, David Adjaye

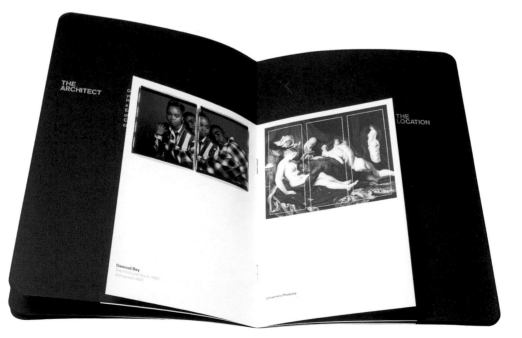

THE
ARCHITECT

THE
LOCATION

Dawoud Bey

Johannes Phokela

A Sense of Place

This is a brochure created by Untitled design studio for the 'Sense of Place' project at international photographic arts agency Autograph ABP. The brochure features black pages that are printed with silver type. Gloss, colour pages have been tipped-in to the brochure and this provides a contrast of both stocks and levels of reflectivity.

Print & Finish Tipping-in and tipping-on

Client: Merchant

Design: NB: Studio

Technical overview:

Tipped-in contents page
and mail-in form

Print & Finish Substrates

Merchant

This is a handbook created by NB: Studio for Merchant, a company that produces annual reports for corporate organisations. The handbook's contents page and a perforated mail-return form at the back of the publication are both tipped-in. This enables a variation of coloured stocks to be used, which then clearly indicates a different type of information. It also allows the mail-return form to be on a heavier stock.

Client: Established & Sons
Design: MadeThought
Technical overview:
Tipped-in invitations

Established & Sons

This brochure was produced for British design and manufacturing company Established & Sons by MadeThought design studio. Invitations to a showcase of Established & Sons' work were tipped-in between the brochure's pages. This technique allows different printing techniques to be used in different parts of a publication. The lower image on this page shows a tipped-in metallic print, while above, a tip-in with different coloured stock reinforces the hierarchy of information.

Print & Finish Tipping-in and tipping-on

Duplexing

Duplexing refers to the bonding of two substrates to form a single one. This allows a stock to have different colours, textures and finishes on each side.

Duplexing also increases the weight of a stock. Two duplexed 270gsm boards would produce a 540gsm substrate, for example.

Front

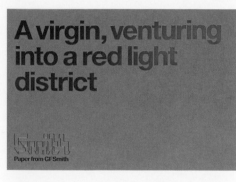

Reverse

Paper from GF Smith
the new collection

GF Smith would like
to invite you to an evening
of drinks, canapés and a
talk by SEA and John Ross

27 January 2005
6.30—9pm
The Fruitmarket Gallery
45 Market Street
Edinburgh EH1 1DF

RSVP
Geoff Burrows
GF Smith
Lockwood Street
Hull HU2 0HL

Telephone
01482 323 503
Facsimile
01482 223 174
Email
gwburrows@gfsmith.com

Edinburgh

This is Colorplan 270gsm Pristine White, litho printed and duplexed to a 270gsm Colorplan Fuchsia Pink with a metallic red foil – finished weight 540gsm.

Front

Reverse

GF Smith

These invitations were created by SEA Design for paper manufacturer GF Smith and use duplexed substrates. The invitation shown on the opposite page is nubuck-brown stock with a silk-weave emboss that is bonded to an orange leatherette embossed board. Pictured above (top) is a pristine white stock duplexed to a fuchsia pink board and (bottom) a lavender stock duplexed to a candy-pink one.

Client: GF Smith
Design: SEA Design
Technical overview:
Duplexed substrates used
as invitations and product
announcements

Metallic, pearlescent,
tissue, iridescent, felt
marked, corrugated,
bible paper, onionskin,
parchment, press board,
archival, embossed,
translucent, coloured
tissue, glassine, surface
enhanced papers,
boards & envelopes.

Print & Finish Duplexing

Client: Self Published
Design: Untitled
Technical overview:
Different stocks finished with
foil blocks and varnishes

Printing

Printing is a collective term that refers to the various different techniques used to apply ink to a substrate or stock. These include: offset lithography, screen printing, gravure (or intaglio), letterpress, hot-metal, lino-cut, thermography, ink-jet and laser printing among others. Each method has its own variables such as printing speed, the available range of colours or printing capacity, in addition to cost. Different printing methods will produce different finishes on the stock. For example, a black-and-white laser printer can produce a flyer to a legible standard, but it does not leave type indentation in the stock, which would occur with letterpress printing.

The printing process is often overlooked when a job is being designed for print, but the designer should take into account the printing process to ensure that the visual impact is optimised and to effectively manage schedule and budgetary constraints.

This section highlights a number of projects that have been creatively enhanced by the wide range of effects that different printing processes can supply.

Untitled (left)

This series of self-promotional cards was created by Untitled design studio. Each card uses a different stock and employs a variety of finishing techniques, such as foil blocks and varnishes, to create an array of interesting effects. Notice how the varnishes reflect the light and catch the eye.

Lithography and CTP
The lithographic printing process uses a treated metal plate to transfer (offset) a design via a rubber blanket to the stock.

Offset lithography is a high-volume and speedy process that produces consistently clean results. Sheet-fed, offset litho presses are typically four-colour. Offset web litho presses use a continuous roll of paper, which allows an even higher printing volume.

This is a multi-colour, offset lithography printing press with single-sheet feed. Each of the grey towers contains a set of plates and rollers that print a different colour on to the substrate.

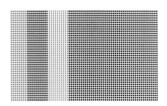

Halftones

A series of screens containing halftone dots are used to replicate the continuous photographic tones in the print process. Once printed, these dots give the illusion of a full-colour image. If the screen angles of each colour were the same, as shown in the illustration above, interference is created and this results in muddled colours. For this reason each colour's screen is offset, or angled, differently. Each colour that will print is screened to produce its own series of halftone dots that will be used to make the printing plate for that colour.

This greyscale image (bottom left) has been printed with a single coarse halftone screen. A duotone has two screens; the one printed below is made using black and magenta. A tritone uses three screens, and all four are used in four-colour printing. The four-colour black image shown below uses all the CMYK plates to create a richer and fuller monotone colour.

Greyscale

Duotone

Four-colour image

Four-colour black

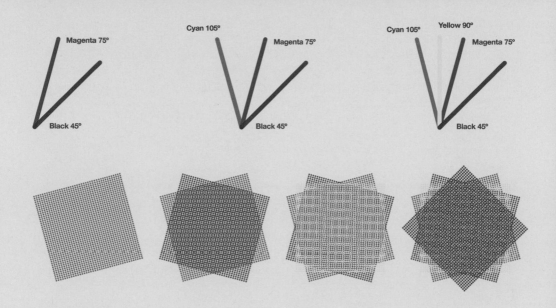

Screen angles

Each of the four process colours has standard screen angles (black 45 degrees, magenta 75 degrees, yellow 90 degrees and cyan 105 degrees). The use of different angles prevents screen interference and the development of moiré patterns, and results in clear colours and the ability to reproduce a four-colour image.

When printing in two colours, for example black and any other process or special colour, each will be set at different angles. The black will be screened at 45 degrees, as this angle is the least obvious to the human eye and black is the strongest colour, and the second colour will be screened at 75 degrees. This principle follows all the way to four-colour printing, and indeed, if a fifth colour is added, it will be given an alternative screen angle to the other four colours.

Moiré

A moiré pattern occurs when the dots of two screens interfere, creating what is referred to as a basket-weave pattern. The group of images above represent screens that have been set at the wrong angles, which allows moiré patterns to develop. The image on the far right uses screens correctly set as cyan 105 degrees and magenta 75 degrees, which produces an image with no moiré.

Computer-to-plate

Computer-to-plate (CTP) is a process that creates a printing plate directly from an electronic file, rather than producing one from printing film. The use of CTP does open up advanced printing possibilities. As the plates are made directly from electronic files rather than film, there is one less process involved, which means a higher resolution is possible. This transfer is also carried out in a sterile environment that reduces contamination from dust and environmental factors.

Dot gain

Dot gain describes the enlarging of ink dots on the printing stock and is something that occurs naturally as the ink is absorbed into the stock. As a consequence, dot gain is more pronounced with a more absorbent paper such as newsprint. Coated stocks contain a fine clay coating which has low ink absorbency and so results in clear, sharp image reproduction.

Screen ruling

The line illustrations and photographs shown below are presented with three common screen ruling values: 60 (coarse), 133 (general purpose) and 175 (high-quality printing, like this book). Lower values give a more open screen with less detail, but this may be preferable depending upon the stock being used for printing. When printing on uncoated stocks that are more absorbent, such as the woodfree section in this book (pages 65–80), lower-value screens are used so that dot gain does not result in a saturated looking image.

60 lpi

133 lpi

175 lpi

1%	2%	3%	4%	5%	6%	7%	8%	9%	10%
1%	2%	3%	4%	5%	6%	7%	8%	9%	10%
1%	2%	3%	4%	5%	6%	7%	8%	9%	10%
1%	2%	3%	4%	5%	6%	7%	8%	9%	10%

Low-value tints

CTP offers higher resolution possibilities and so is able to reproduce finer and more delicate tints than traditional printing methods. Normally the minimum effective tint level is around 8–10%. In the strips above (C,M,Y and K) the extent to which finer tints can be applied using CTP is demonstrated. Notice that yellow is the lightest colour, and therefore tints of this colour disappear, or fail to register, sooner than the other, more saturated colours.

Reversing out

As CTP uses a random dot placement method, which places each dot where it should go (rather than placing it on an x-y coordinate), smoother lines are generated with finer resolutions, and with fewer jagged edges. However, lines finer than 0.25mm will still present problems particularly when angled or reversing out text, when it will start to break up.

When reversing out it is best to stick to simple linear fonts and increase font weight to compensate for creep. Letter spacing also needs to be increased to further compensate – as optically the letterforms will look closer together as the ink spreads.

With CTP it is possible to reproduce type at small sizes, although the use of fine or intricate typefaces should be avoided, as these will not be be legible under less than 2pt.

With CTP it is possible to reproduce type at small sizes, although the use of fine or intricate typefaces should be avoided, as these will not be be legible under less than 3pt.

With CTP it is possible to reproduce type at small sizes, although the use of fine or intricate typefaces should be avoided, as these will not be be legible under less than 4pt.

With CTP it is possible to reproduce type at small sizes, although the use of fine or intricate typefaces should be avoided, as these will not be be legible under less than 5pt.

With CTP it is possible to reproduce type at small sizes, although the use of fine or intricate typefaces should be avoided, as these will not be be legible under less than 8pt.

1pt .75pt .5pt .25pt .15pt .1pt 1pt .75pt .5pt .25pt .15pt .1pt

Wash printing

Wash printing is a special technique that allows the most delicate of colours to be applied to a substrate.

Wash printing uses ink that has been heavily diluted in order to produce a flat colour that is more subtle than light special colours such as pastels. This wash is applied by pre-printing the sheets with a flood-colour of the diluted ink.

If this colour was applied as part of the four-colour process, it would print with a halftone dot, as shown below. Wash printing allows a subtle, sophisticated approach to colour application.

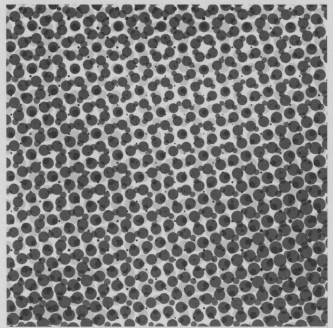

Unless printed as a special, flat areas of colour, such as the small square above, are made from halftone dots of the four process colours.

Brick-work (right)

Brick-work was created by Cartlidge Levene design studio for Sergison Bates architects. The publication features grey tipped-in pages. This subtle, flat grey is produced using a wash print with a watered-down ink to give a fine, light base colour. The first printing pass supplies this solid base colour, and then the stock follows a second, standard pass.

Client: Sergison Bates
Design: Cartlidge Levene
Technical overview:
Wash print to give light base
colour to tipped-in sections

Silk-screen printing
Silk-screen printing imposes an image on to a substrate by forcing ink through a screen that contains the design.

Screen printing is not a high-volume printing method because each colour that is applied to the substrate has to dry before another can be applied, but it is a flexible method which can be used to apply a design to virtually any substrate. Silk-screen printing allows more viscous inks to be used, which can provide additional tactile qualities to a piece of work.

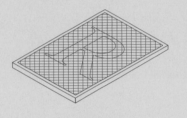

The pattern to be reproduced is fixed to a screen in such a way that ink can pass through the screen's mesh in those areas that are to be printed. The screen frame is placed over the substrate.

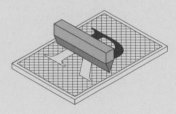

A squeegee is used to draw the printing ink over the screen, pressing it through the design and on to the substrate.

The screen is carefully removed to reveal the design that has been applied to the substrate.

Housing Services (right)

This folder for the University of the Arts, London, was created by Turnbull Grey design studio. The greyboard folder has been silk-screen printed in three colours (red, yellow and white). The tactile, natural feel of the greyboard is augmented by the solid and intense colours, which also enhance the tactile qualities of the piece.

Client: University of the
Arts, London
Design: Turnbull Grey
Technical overview: Silk-
screen printed greyboard

HOUSING
SERVICES

UNIVERSITY OF THE ARTS
LONDON CAMBERWELL COLLEGE OF ARTS
CENTRAL SAINT MARTINS COLLEGE OF ART
AND DESIGN CHELSEA COLLEGE OF ART AND
DESIGN LONDON COLLEGE OF COMMUNICATION
LONDON COLLEGE OF FASHION

Print & Finish Silk-screen printing

Letterpress printing

Letterpress is a method of relief printing whereby an inked, raised surface is pressed against the substrate.

Letterpress was the first form of commercial printing, and much print-specific terminology derives from it. The raised surface that makes the impression is typically made from pieces of type, but photo-engraved plates can also be used. Letterpress printing can often be identified by the slight indentation made into the substrate.

A selection of letterpress characters made from wood.

A defect of letterpress printing is that the impression from the raised surface varies every time it is pressed against a substrate, giving the characters a uniqueness where each is subtly different, which is appealing to designers. This defect has become a popular style, to the extent that an original design is printed letterpress, and the result is scanned and reproduced in offset lithography to produce multiple copies of it.

These letterpress characters demonstrate the sort of natural defects that occur on each printed impression.

Self-promotional Brochure (right)

This is a cover to a self-promotional brochure by Turnbull Grey design studio, which is printed in an extended slab-serif typeface by letterpress. Each letter has a distinctive quality because every character block has taken and transferred the ink slightly differently, which means that each book produced is unique.

Client: Self Published
Design: Turnbull Grey
Technical overview:
Extended slab-serif type
printed letterpress

We must always remind ourselves this: philosophy is an art form, a literary genre like poetry and fiction. The philosopher moves his concepts around on the page, just like the novelist manipulates his characters, he's certainly not producing science. But everything indicates that it is an art form in deplorable decline.

In a 21st century obsessed with utility, philosophy seems to be permanently confined to the dusty corridors of academia, where a handful of pale nerds spend their days tirelessly twisting and turning technicalities inherited from Hegel or Kant. And nobody in the outside world cares one iota. From a creative point of view, the art of philosophy seems dead.

But academia is hardly the right place to look for literary creativity; philosophy is actually doing just fine under various guises in the most surprising places. Remember that whenever we step outside the confines of our regular world view and start to question ourselves and our habitual perceptions of things, we instantly start doing philosophy. We establish a meta level, we think about thinking in a language about language.

Consequently, philosophy can, properly understood, capture the attention of a huge audience. It just isn't marketed very well at present. That could change quickly, however. We just need to remove three major misconceptions.

1. Philosophy is not an academic discipline. To take a professor of philosophy for a philosopher proper would be like regarding a professor of literature as a novelist or poet. Only rarely do these two separate functions coincide. This means, of course, that most of the relevant philosophy today is produced outside university departments, where they rather do the history of philosophy in the form of endless commentary.

A practical rule of thumb is: if a book has footnotes in it, it is anything but philosophy. It is an academic text, not art. Proper philosophy should have no more footnotes in it than fiction or poetry (Elliot is the exception that confirms this rule).

2. Philosophy is not science. Scientific rules simply do not apply. Philosophy proves nothing, and the utility value is zero, as is the case with poetry and fiction. In fact, the whole idea that human actions should be valued according to the amount of utility they produce, is itself a philosophical idea, called utilitarianism, in desperate need of philosophical scrutiny.

3. Philosophy is going big! Not in the sense of becoming omnipotent and dictating in detail how people should live their lives and build their societies. That would just amount to old-fashioned political ideology.

But big rather in the same sense that Big Science is big: aiming for a grand theory of everything. Which in the case of philosophy means a grand theory uniting the individual and collective subjects. And let's not forget that whatever Big Science comes up with, it will need Big Philosophy to work out and define the new and expanded world view that would have to accommodate a scientific theory of everything.

The philosophy of the last century, from Nietzsche via Wittgenstein to the postmodernists of the 1980s and 1990s, should be viewed as one big deconstruction project, an endeavour to expose the weaknesses and contradictions of the rationalist paradigm and the remaining residues of the Enlightenment. But now we have reached the end of the line. There is nothing more to deconstruct, and we must not be too timid to admit it. In fact, philosophy is now beginning to move in a different direction, redefining what it means to be human, or even trans-human, in a world of interactive communication and virtual communities.

This new development should actually come as no surprise. The whole deconstructionist rage of the last century makes perfect sense when you think if it as a big house-cleaning the day before the party guests arrive. With all the shortcomings of rationalism removed, philosophy is back in good shape, ready for new adventures. And as always in the history of philosophy, the new direction is one that nobody would have expected, least of all the discarded and gloomy postmodernists themselves. The new generation of superstar thinkers – like Slavoj Zizek, Brian Massumi, Simon Critchley, and The Scandinavians – take their cues from newscasts, movie scripts and quantum physics rather than from the annals of old philosophy.

Every major transformation of information technology has, given time for absorption, caused a revolution of the mind. The reason why the ancient Greeks were able to establish philosophy as a discourse was certainly not some sort of outstanding intelligence, but simply that the organisation of society – mainly determined by the dominant mode of communication – created the first social class in history with sufficient time and means to reflect on human existence in debate and in writing. So the Greeks took what had been imported from Egypt, Babylonia and Persia, and created a new art form. Philosophy had arrived.

The next revolution occurred in Europe in the 17th and 18th centuries. The invention of the printing press had changed the feudal society completely and gave birth to a whole new class, the urban bourgeoisie, and a new demand for information and social critique. The result was the shock to the system of thought since then referred to as the Enlightenment.

And now, with the arrival of interactive information technology, the framework for social power structures and thought patterns change drastically. While the mass media obsess over the all-new gadgets, philosophy is interested in the social and cultural implications of interactivity. Nothing could be more important, since the revolution in technology inevitably will bring about a crisis of traditional values, politics, social institutions, etc. It's already happening, and it's called globalisation.

Economic and financial globalisation must be followed by a globalisation of culture and politics, since the concept of a national culture is becoming increasingly irrelevant and national politics increasingly impotent. This is the impulse for the art of philosophy to leave the deconstructionist phase behind, to start making sense of all the rapid changes, to speculate on the shape of the global political order and to give it some credibility. Add to this the ongoing revolution in scientific fields like cosmology, quantum physics and biology: we are entering a new enlightenment, and Big Philosophy is where it is all coming together.

Client: Zembla
Design: Frost Design
Technical overview:
Woodtype form with text reversed out

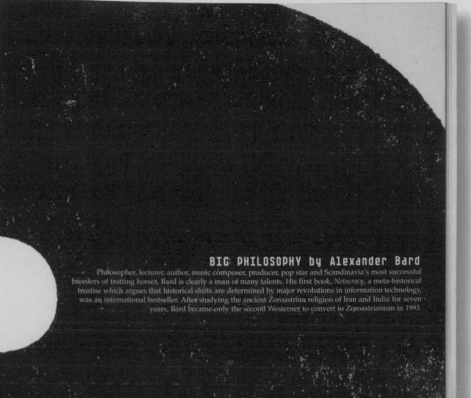

BIG PHILOSOPHY by Alexander Bard

Philosopher, lecturer, author, music composer, producer, pop star and Scandinavia's most successful breeders of trotting horses, Bard is clearly a man of many talents. His first book, *Netocracy*, a meta-historical treatise which argues that historical shifts are determined by major revolutions in information technology, was an international bestseller. After studying the ancient Zoroastrian religion of Iran and India for seven years, Bard became only the second Westerner to convert to Zoroastrianism in 1993.

Zembla

This is a double-page spread from *Zembla* magazine, which was created by Frost Design. The design was created using a letter character that was letterpress printed from a wood block, which was then digitised and reproduced in offset lithography. The text is reversed out of the black ink to appear white.

Reversed out

Reversed out refers to a rendition of text or image printed on a black (or dark) colour background.

The white text or image is effectively 'cut' out of the colour of the design underneath it.

Hot-metal printing

Hot-metal printing, also know as hot-type composition or cast metal, refers to the process of casting type in lines of molten metal.

Text is typed into a machine to produce a punched paper tape, which controls the characters that are cast by the casting machine. Hot-metal type allows the production of large quantities of type in a relatively inexpensive fashion.

Movable type is a method that uses single type characters, which are set in a block and printed. As each character is a single unit, it is 'movable' and so can be used again and again.

A piece of movable type.

A tray of movable type characters in a printer's workshop. All the characters in the tray correspond to a particular typeface.

Movable type characters that have been locked into position in a chase or metal frame to produce a printed page.

Gavin Martin Associates (right)

This is a change-of-address card produced by design agency NB: Studio for Gavin Martin Associates. The company had relocated to the Tea Building in Shoreditch, London. Hot-metal printing was used to leave a heavy imprint in an uncoated stock, which provided a subtle, but direct, connection to the printing profession of the client. Each card was individually stained with a tea ring to link to the printer's new location and make every one unique. The cards carried the credit 'Printed in England using Darjeeling. Brewed by NB: Studio'.

Client: Gavin Martin
Associates
Design: NB: Studio
Technical overview:
Metal type on uncoated stock
with randomised tea stains

Gavin Martin Associates have moved...
Unit 4.05 The Tea Building
56 Shoreditch High Street
London E1 6JJ
T:020 7729 0091 F:020 7729 9872
www.gavinmartin.co.uk

Printed in England using Darjeeling
Brewed by NB Studio

Gavin Martin Associates have moved...
Unit 4.05 The Tea Building
56 Shoreditch High Street
London E1 6JJ
T:020 7729 0091 F:020 7729 9872
www.gavinmartin.co.uk

Printed in England using Darjeeling
Brewed by NB Studio

Gavin Martin Associates have moved...
Unit 4.05 The Tea Building
56 Shoreditch High Street
London E1 6JJ
T:020 7729 0091 F:020 7729 9872
www.gavinmartin.co.uk

Printed in England using Darjeeling
Brewed by NB Studio

Gavin Martin Associates have moved...
Unit 4.05 The Tea Building
56 Shoreditch High Street
London E1 6JJ
T:020 7729 0091 F:020 7729 9872
www.gavinmartin.co.uk

Printed in England using Darjeeling
Brewed by NB Studio

Thermography

Thermography is an in-line print finishing process that is used to produce raised lettering on paper substrates.

Thermographic powder is deposited on to a sheet of printed paper (from an offset press) while the ink is still wet. The powder sticks to the wet ink, and fuses to it when the substrate is passed through an oven, which leaves a raised surface with a mottled texture, as seen in the detail below. The process can also be used with letterpress printing.

Lisa Pritchard Agency (above and right)

This is a Christmas card created by SEA Design for the Lisa Pritchard Agency. The text has been thermographically printed to provide raised, 'bubbly' characters that are highly visible, very tactile and reflect light in a unique way.

Client: Lisa Pritchard Agency
Design: SEA Design
Technical overview:
Thermographic printing to give
raised, mottled characters

SEASONS GREET
INGS FROM RICH
ARD BRADBURY/
NICK DALY/IGOR
EMMERICH/LAUR
ENCE HASKELL/N
ANCY HONEY/TO
NY MCGEE

LPA/

Tactile
Designers often select printing methods that will introduce a tactile quality to their design so that people can
feel it as well as see it. Thermography, screen-printing and embossing all provide this additional element.

Lino-cut printing

Lino cut is a low-volume, relief-printing method in which an image is cut into a thin piece of linoleum that is inked and mounted on to a piece of wood. The wood is then pressed against a substrate, and must be re-inked for every impression. The method was used by artists Henri Matisse and Pablo Picasso.

The image cut out of the linoleum is the reverse, or mirror image of the desired final design. The lino cut is in essence the negative from which the positive is printed.

Paw Prints (right)

This is the cover of an illustrated, self-published book called *Paw Prints,* which was produced by design studio Webb & Webb. The red stripes on the cover and the book's illustrations were printed using the lino-cut method. The typography was reproduced by letterpress and the cover substrate is duplexed with a combination of paper board and endpapers. Lino-cut printing produces a unique impression each time due to the variations in ink-film thickness and application pressure.

Client: Self Published
Design: Webb & Webb
Technical overview:
Combination of lino-cut and
letterpress printing

PAW PRINTS

A Story by Holly Skeet

Pictures by Chris Brown

Hand & Eye Editions

Client: RSA
Design: Untitled
Technical overview:
Black varnish on black
substrate produces striking
visual appearance

Finishing

Print finishing encompasses a wide range of processes that can provide the final touches to a design once the substrate has been printed. These processes include die cutting, embossing, debossing, foil blocking, varnishing and screen printing to name but a few, and can transform an ordinary looking piece into something much more arresting.

Finishing processes can add decorative elements to a printed piece, such as the shimmer of a foil block, or textural qualities, such as those produced by an emboss or deboss. Finishing techniques can also provide added functionality to a design, and even be a constituent part of a publication's format. For example, a die cut alters the physical product, perhaps changing its shape or providing an aperture through which other parts of the publication can be viewed.

Although the application of print-finishing techniques signals the end of the production process, these techniques should not be considered as afterthoughts, but as an integral part of a design, and one that needs to be considered during the planning stage.

Art for Architecture (left)

This is an invitation created by Untitled design studio for the Art for Architecture annual event, which is hosted by the Royal Society of Arts in the UK. The invitation features a black varnish that is applied in a halftone pattern on to a black substrate, which produces a very striking and arresting result.

Varnishes

A varnish is a colourless coating that is often applied to a printed piece to protect the substrate from scuffing, wear or smudging. Varnish can also be used to enhance the visual appearance of a design, or elements within it. Varnish can produce three finishes – gloss, dull and satin – and, while not strictly a varnish, UV coating can also be used to add decorative touches to designs.

Applying a varnish increases colour absorption and speeds up the drying process. By 'locking in' the printing ink under a protective coat, the varnish helps to prevent the ink rubbing off when the substrate is handled.

Varnish can be applied in-line or 'wet'; which essentially means it is treated as an additional colour during the printing process. A wet layer of varnish is applied on to a wet layer of ink, and both are absorbed into the stock as they dry, which reduces the visual impact of the varnish. An off-line varnish is applied once the printing inks have dried, and therefore less is absorbed by the stock. Varnish performs better on coated substrates, again because less is absorbed by the stock.

Varnishes can be used to produce different effects; as these details (above and opposite) taken from examples on the following pages, demonstrate.
Above, left to right: spot UV, clear and pearlescent varnishes.
Opposite, left to right: spot UV, lamination and black varnish.

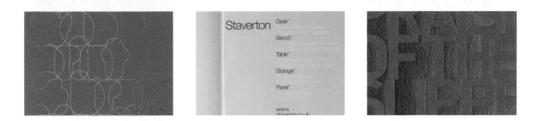

Gloss
A gloss varnish reflects back light and is frequently used to enhance the appearance of photographs or other graphic elements in brochures, as it adds to the sharpness and saturation of images.

Matt (or dull)
A matt varnish is typically used with text-heavy pages to diffuse light, reduce glare and so increase readability. It gives a non-glossy, smooth finish to the printed page.

Satin (or silk)
A satin varnish is a middle option between the gloss and matt varnishes. It provides some highlight, but is not as flat as a matt finish.

Neutral
Machine sealing is the application of a basic, almost invisible, coating that seals the printing ink without affecting the appearance of the job. It is often used to accelerate the drying of fast turnaround print jobs (such as leaflets) on matt and satin papers, upon which inks dry more slowly.

UV varnish
UV varnish is a clear liquid that is applied like ink and cured instantly with ultraviolet light. It can provide either a gloss or matt coating. Increasingly, UV varnish is used as a spot covering to highlight a particular image because it provides more shine than varnish.

Full-bleed UV
The most common type of all-over UV coating, largely because it produces a very high gloss effect.

Spot UV
The varnish is applied to highlight discrete areas of a printed design, both visually and by imparting a different texture. The effect of spot UV can by maximised when it is applied over matt-laminated printing.

Textured spot UV
Textures can be created with spot UV varnish to provide an additional tactile quality to a print piece. Examples of textured spot UV varnish effects include sandpaper, leather, crocodile skin and raised.

Pearlescent
A varnish that subtly reflects myriad colours to give a luxurious effect.

Client: Marsh Mercer
Design: Turnbull Grey
Technical overview:
Text reversed out of a
pearlescent varnish that retains
ease of legibility

Client: E A Shaw
Design: Four Letter Word
Technical overview:
UV spot varnish grid of initials

BE MOVED

E A Shaw (above)

This brochure was designed by Four Letter Word for London estate agent
E A Shaw. The cover of the brochure features a UV spot varnish of the lower
case 'i' and 'h' initials of the property development project name (Ingram House),
which were arranged in a grid pattern against a plain red background. The effect
is subtle yet eye-catching.

Marsh Mercer (left)

This invitation was created by Turnbull Grey design studio for risk specialist
Marsh Mercer. It features text which is printed in a pearlescent varnish and can
only be read clearly when it catches the light in a certain way. The main text
elements are printed in a slab-serif type and a large point size to facilitate reading.

Client: RSA
Design: Untitled
Technical overview:
Clear varnish and emboss
to create tactile surface

Parent (right)

This is a calling card created by Parent design studio that features a UV varnish applied on black Plike, a plastic-like paper stock. The varnish reflects the light and highlights the subtle outlines of the custom typeface, which reads 'Parent design for web print & brand identity'.

Outside (left)

This is an invitation produced for the Royal Society of Arts by Untitled design studio. The design is screen printed on to greyboard stock, embossed and given a clear varnish coating. The varnish gives the screen print extra prominence and highlights the contrasting rough texture of the board, while giving a tactile difference in the surface.

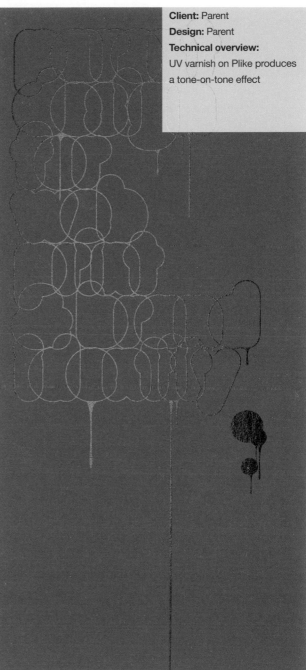

Client: Parent
Design: Parent
Technical overview:
UV varnish on Plike produces a tone-on-tone effect

Staverton

This brochure was created by SEA Design for office furniture company Staverton. The brochure is laminated, which gives it a high-gloss effect. Shown below is an impressive four-panel gatefold that the brochure contains.

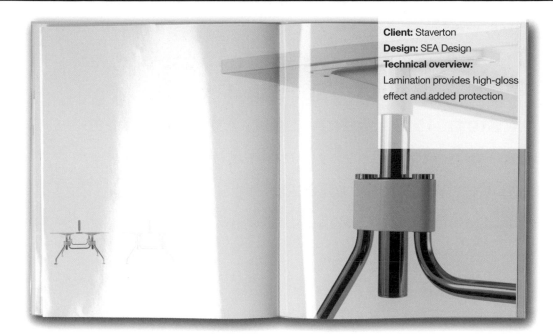

Client: Staverton
Design: SEA Design
Technical overview:
Lamination provides high-gloss effect and added protection

Die cut

Die cutting is a process that uses a steel die to cut away a specified section of a design. It is mainly used for decorative purposes and to enhance the visual performance of a piece.

In addition to altering the shape of a design for visual enhancement, a die cut can serve a functional purpose such as creating an aperture that allows a user to see inside or through a publication.

The cards (left) are part of the Acorn project shown on the facing page, and share the same floral motif. The cards have die-cut rounded corners, which both softens their visual appearance and replicates the generous curves of the upper case 'A' in the main design.

Acorn (above and right)

These designs were created by Studio Output for conceptual textiles company Acorn. A die cut in the cover in the shape of an upper case 'A' (for Acorn) provides a view of the material inside, and this lends the piece depth and texture as the colours from the interior sheets are seen through the aperture. The die-cut cover reflects the floral theme of the content as the counter of the 'A' is designed as a sprig of leaves. The inner sheets are softened, in line with the floral themes they display, as they incorporate die-cut rounded corners.

Client: Acorn
Design: Studio Output
Technical overview:
Die-cut cover design and page
corners, flower theme
incorporated throughout

Acorn
Spring + Summer Collection '05
Conceptual Textiles

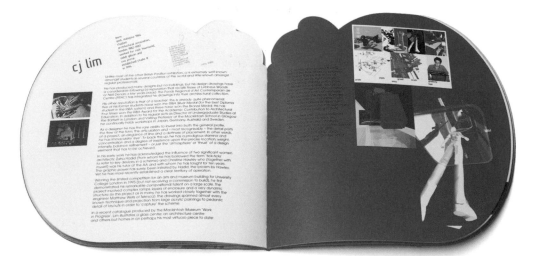

Client: British Council

Design: Studio Myerscough

Technical overview:

Die cut gives shape of

cover element

Nine Positions (above)

This is a brochure that was created by Studio Myerscough for Nine Positions
an exhibition curated by Peter Cook for the ninth Venice Biennale of Architecture.
The publication is die cut so that it takes the shape of the stem of the yellow '9'
which is printed in a stencil font on the greyboard cover.

Museon (right)

This is a greetings card created by Faydherbe / De Vringer design studio, which
Dutch museum Museon gave to its staff. The circle die cut provides an aperture
through which one can view a coin mounted inside. The coin commemorates the
750th anniversary of The Hague, and features an image of the museum. Removal
of the coin reveals the museum's logo.

Client: Museon
Design:
Faydherbe / De Vringer
Technical overview:
Die-cut aperture inspired by
company identity

MUSEON

Folding
Different folding methods will produce different creative effects and offer different functionality and means of organisation.

Valley fold

Mountain fold

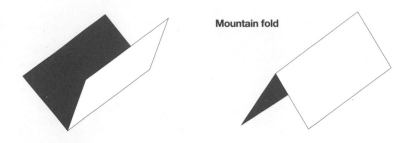

The valley and mountain folds (shown above) are both named after the geographical features they replicate. Both feature a single central fold. Combined, these two folds form the basis of a wide variety of fold combinations (see page 166).

Almeida Theatre by NB: Studio

This invitation for the Almeida Theatre features two die cuts that are perpendicular to the mountain fold. This folding method is called *parallel folding*, and in this instance the parallel fold helps create a seat for the die-cut figure.

Levi's Music Job Club by KesselsKramer

This booklet for clothing label Levi's contains a poster that is folded with a series of valley and mountain folds.

Client: Arnolfini
Design: Thirteen
Technical overview:
Irregular diagonal folds to
create three-dimensional
invitation

Arnolfini (above)

This is an invitation created by design studio Thirteen for the reopening of Bristol's
Arnolfini Gallery following an 18-month closure for architectural redevelopment.
The invitation is produced from a single leaf of Think4 stock that is printed in four
colours and has irregular diagonal valley and mountain folds, which produces a
three-dimensional object.

Print & Finish Folding

Throw outs

A throw out is a folded sheet of paper that is bound into a publication to provide extra space to showcase a particular image or visual element.

To open a throw out, the extra panel is extended horizontally. The sheet will have a slightly smaller dimension than the overall publication so that it can nest comfortably when folded. A throw out is similar to a throw up (shown below right), which when opened is extended vertically.

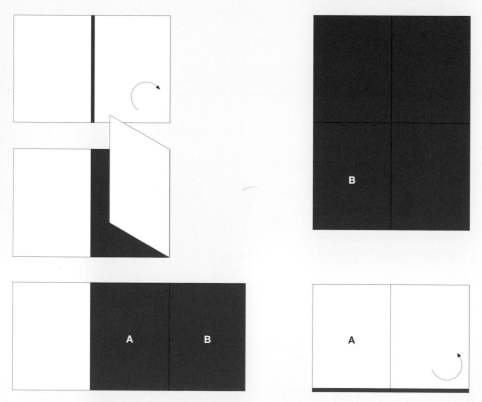

Left: A throw out; the recto page is a double panel page (A and B), which is folded into the spine of the publication. For panel B to nest comfortably in the publication it has to be slightly narrower than panel A. Panel A is narrower than the publication size so that the throw out will not be damaged during the binding and trimming processes.
Right: A throw up sees the spread (A) open up vertically to reveal the concealed content (B).

Client: Blueprint Magazine
Design: George & Vera
Technical overview:
Two-page throw out

Will Alsop
Wilkinson Eyre
ZEDfactory
Future Systems
Eric Kuhne
Ben Kelly
Shin and Tomoko Azumi
Jane Atfield
Priestman Goode
Gerry McGovern
Seymour Powell
Jonathan Ive
Lisa-Dionne Morris
Craig Johnston
George Davies
Ross Lovegrove
Garrick Hamm
Mark Farrow
Martin Lambie-Nairn
Margaret Calvert
David Quay and Freda Sack

Blueprint Magazine

This insert was created by George & Vera design studio for *Blueprint* Magazine.
It features the work of creatives from a variety of design disciplines, including
Margaret Calvert's UK motorway signage scheme, David Quay's and Freda Sack's
Yellow Pages typeface design and Jonathan Ive's iPod design. The insert includes
a two-page throw out.

Gatefold

A gatefold is a sheet with four panels that is placed in the publication so that the left and right panels fold inward with parallel folds and meet at the spine without overlapping.

In the illustration below, the inner panels (B) have the same dimensions as the pages of the publication, but the outer panels (A) are slightly narrower so that they can nest comfortably at the spine. Gatefolds are often used in magazines to provide extra space and are particularly useful for displaying panoramic vista images.

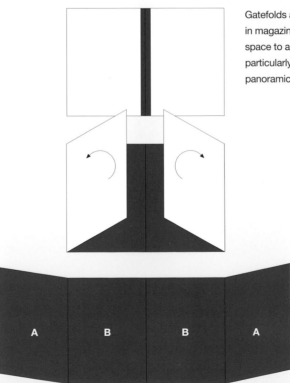

Gatefolds are commonly used in magazines to provide extra space to a key image, and are particularly useful when including panoramic vista images.

Client: Kunst en Bedrijf

Design:

Faydherbe / De Vringer

Technical overview:

Gatefolds provide better
visual representation than
standard format

Pictured bottom is the opened-
out gatefold with the reverse
sides of the folding wings above.
The gatefold's wing panels are
narrower than the central panels
so that they can nest comfortably
when folded into the publication.

Kunst en Bedrijf

This is a promotional brochure created by Faydherbe / De Vringer design studio for
Kunst en Bedrijf (Art and Business), an organisation that acts as an intermediary
between artists and companies (or schools) looking to commission artworks. The
brochure showcases a project that Kunst en Bedrijf managed, and features a gatefold
that presents the reader with a better visual representation of it than would have
otherwise been provided with a standard format.

French fold

A French fold is a sheet of stock that is printed on one side and folded vertically and then horizontally to form a four-page uncut section.

A French fold can also be bound into a printed item (as shown in the illustration below) to give a more substantial feel to the publication's pages. The section is sewn through the (open) binding edge so that the fore- and top edges remain folded and untrimmed. The top edge (A) is trimmed off during the binding process to leave a sealed fore-edge that forms a cavity. The section inner may be printed on.

This standard French fold forms an eight-page section

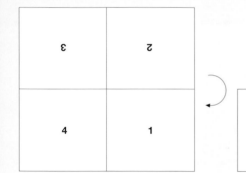

Heavily-filled or coated stocks are prone to cracking on the fore-edge and high-caliper stock may also crack when folded; this makes them unsuitable for French folding. This publication was created by North design studio. The content prints in the cavities of the French fold pages and the publication is printed on bible paper, a stock that will not crack when folded, and will lie flat.

Client: Sweeps
Design: Studio Myerscough
Technical overview:
French fold doubles the
caliper of the page

Sweeps

This is a property brochure created by Studio Myerscough for the Sweeps Building
development in London's Clerkenwell area. The brochure features French fold pages
that add depth and substance to the publication.

This French fold will be perfect bound to create pages that have a cavity.

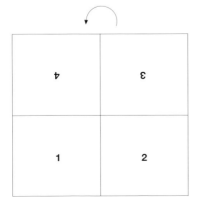

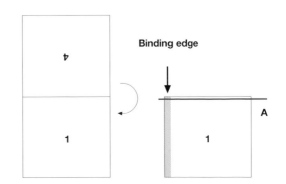

Concertina fold

A concertina (or accordion) fold comprises two or more parallel folds that go in opposite directions and open out. This folding method enables many pages to be collapsed into a smaller size publication.

A concertina-folded document can be opened from either the left or right side. As a reader can open a concertina folded document at any point, the content needs to be coherent both when it is opened out and as a separate series of spreads.

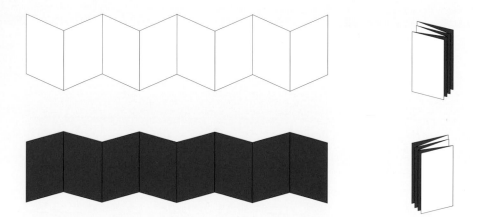

This illustration shows the alternating valley and mountain folds of a concertina fold, and how the size of the publication is reduced when folded.

John Robertson Architects (right)

This is a name-change announcement card, which was created by designer Gavin Ambrose for architectural firm John Robertson. The 12-page publication features a concertina fold that turns the publication into a structure. It features a spot UV varnish that is applied to a matt laminate, which is printed with a metallic silver ink.

Client: John Robertson
Architects
Design: Gavin Ambrose
Technical overview:
Concertina fold creates
structural properties

Roll fold

A roll fold is composed of a series of parallel valley folds, which are further folded in to one another.

As the reader opens a roll-folded document the content is gradually revealed panel by panel. In this way, the fold functions like a slow reveal. For a large document or rigid substrate, the panels may need to be of successively larger widths so that they can nest comfortably.

However, as with a concertina fold, the content contained within a roll-folded piece needs to read as a series of spreads in addition to a continuous strip. Roll folds can be used to good effect as a frieze graphic as the opened-out example below shows.

The document comprises a strip with several panels. Successive parallel valley folds are performed so that the document rolls up.

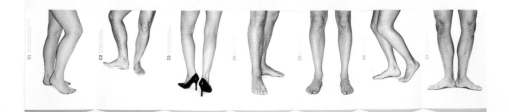

Christmas Card

This card, 'stocking fillers', was created by Turnbull Ripley design studio. It features seven black-and-white photographs of pairs of legs. The photographs are enclosed and hidden by a roll fold so that only the metallic gold outer is immediately visible. To view the photographs the reader unrolls the publication like a stocking is unrolled.

Client: Self published
Design: Turnbull Ripley
Technical overview:
Roll fold to conceal content

Embossing and debossing

An emboss or deboss is a design that is stamped into a substrate with ink or foil, which results in a three-dimensional, raised, decorative or textured surface to provide emphasis to certain elements of a design. Generally, a paper stock with a thicker caliper holds an emboss (or deboss) much better than thinner stocks.

Embossing
A raised impression made in conjunction *with* ink or foil on the embossed image.

Blind embossing
A raised impression made *without* using ink or foil on the embossed image.

Debossing
A recessed impression made in conjunction *with* ink or foil on the debossed image.

Blind debossing
A recessed impression made *without* using ink or foil on the debossed image.

30/30 Vision (right)

This cover was created by Turnbull Grey design studio for 30/30 Vision: Creative Journeys in Contemporary Craft, an event held by the the UK's Crafts Council. The cover features an abstract floral pattern made from small debossed circles.

Client: Crafts Council
Design: Turnbull Grey
Technical overview:
Abstract pattern with
debossed circles

Print & Finish Embossing and debossing

Client: The Dutch Ministry of Health, Welfare and Sport
Design:
Faydherbe / De Vringer
Technical overview:
Embossed lettering with UV lacquer

Zorg van Betekenis (above)

This is a brochure created by Faydherbe / De Vringer design studio for the Dutch Ministry of Health, Welfare and Sport. *Zorg Van Betekenis* (Care With Significance) features a retrospective view on ten years of quality management and points for future attention.

The design is based on the identity card that is needed to receive care in Dutch hospitals. The cover typography has been embossed and covered with a UV lacquer. A small percentage of blue was added to the orange lettering to give better contrast against the white background.

Crafts Council (right)

This is the cover of a calendar that was created by Turnbull Grey design studio for the UK's Crafts Council. The cover features a deep deboss into a flock substrate, which is complemented by a silver foil block for the lettering.

Client: Crafts Council
Design: Turnbull Grey
Technical overview:
Deboss into flock with silver
foil block lettering

CRAFTS COUNCIL
THE NATIONAL CENTRE FOR CONTEMPORARY CRAFTS

Foil blocking

Foil blocking is a process whereby coloured foil is pressed on to a substrate via a heated die, which causes the foil to separate from its backing. The foil is a thin polyester film containing a dry pigment. Several terms are used to describe this process including foil stamp, heat stamp, hot stamp, block print and foil emboss.

Flat stamping

A basic flat stamp that gives a slight raise above the surface and usually no impression on the reverse side of the substrate.

Multi-level stamping

A die created with different levels and textures that can produce elegant designs. Also called sculptured foil embossing, it provides eye-catching results, but is more expensive.

Maddison Business Systems (above and right)

These are details taken from the introductory page of a brochure that was created for Maddison Business Systems by Turnbull Grey design studio. This page of the brochure features foil-blocked type on a blue stock, which results in attractive detailing that imparts a quality feel to the publication.

Client: Maddison
Business Systems
Design: Turnbull Grey
Technical overview:
Foil blocked type on blue
stock imparts quality feel

Print & Finish Foil blocking

Client: Iniva

Design: Untitled

Technical overview:
Silver foil block on plastic substrate

1994–2004
A Decade of Difference

Join us to celebrate *A Decade of Difference* at inIVA's 10th birthday party on Thursday 25 November 2004, 7.00pm till late

60 Exhibitions
25 Research Projects

Blacktronica sound system featuring
Charlie Dark & friends

60 Talks & Conferences
20 Education Projects

T Bar, First Floor, The Tea Building, 56 Shoreditch High Street, London E1 6JJ. *Fully accessible. Lift access via reception*

23 Multimedia Projects
25 Publications

RSVP by 15 November 2004
birthday@iniva.org Tel 020 7729 9616

5,000,000
Website Visitors

Admits one person only
Please bring this invitation with you

1 Invite
1 Party

ARTS COUNCIL ENGLAND   inIVA

A Decade of Difference (above)

This is an invitation created by Untitled design studio for London-based arts agency Iniva. It features a silver foil block and red typography on a clear plastic substrate, in which some of the text seems to disappear as the viewing angle changes.

Future Face (right)

This is the cover of Sandra Kemp's *Future Face*, which was designed by Studio Myerscough for Profile Books. The title of the book is emblazoned across a hyperreal image in an angular font that is silver-foil blocked, which results in a very futuristic effect.

Client: Profile Books
Design: Studio Myerscough
Technical overview:
Silver-foil block title provides
futuristic effect

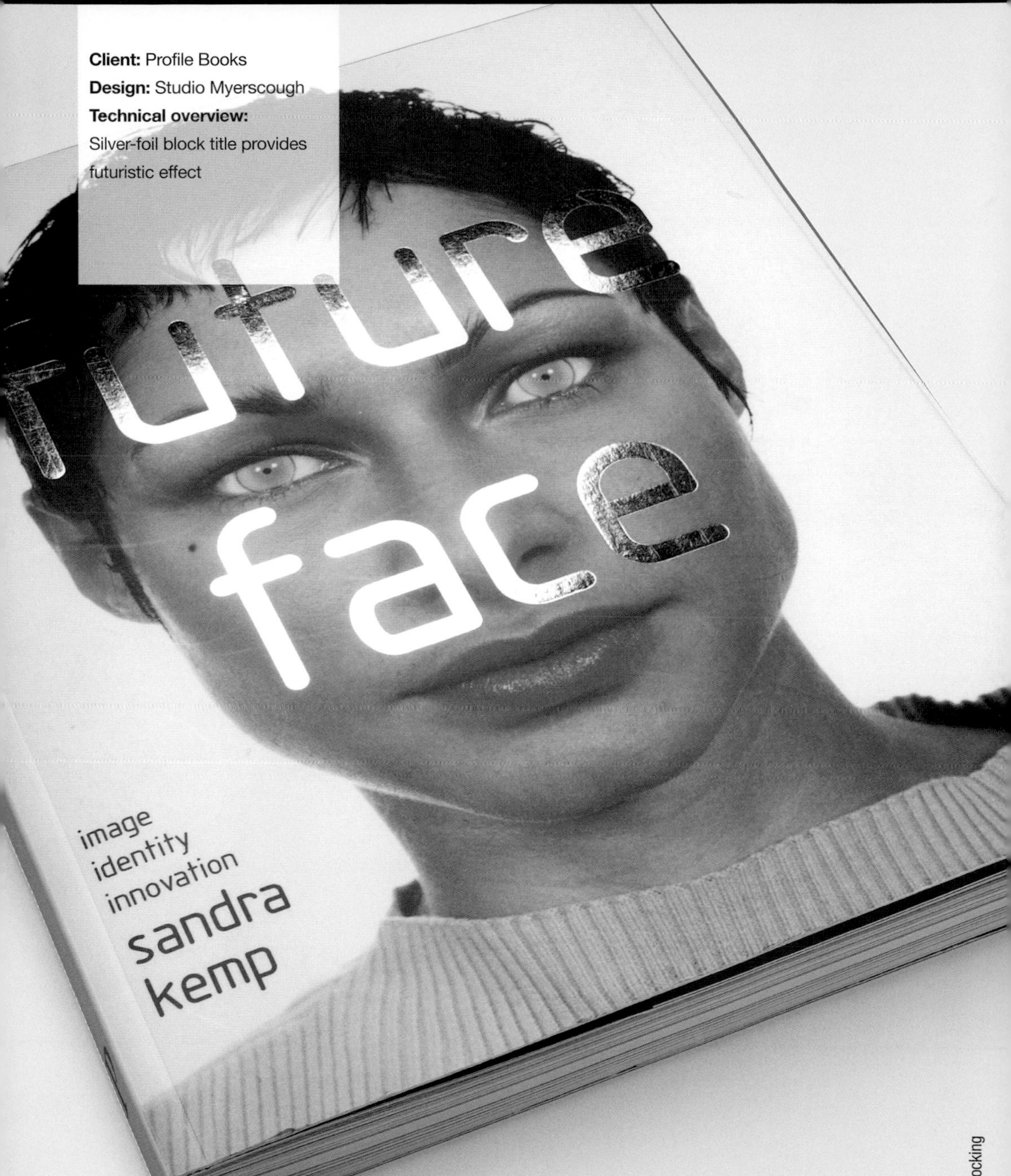

future
face

image
identity
innovation
sandra
kemp

AWARDS CEREMONY 2002

Client: University of the Arts, London

Design: Turnbull Grey

Technical overview: Silver-foil block on flat-coloured stock provides a modern twist

Awards Ceremony

These are silver-foil blocked covers created by Turnbull Grey design studio for an awards ceremony held at London's University of the Arts. Flat-coloured stock and a sans-serif typeface blocked in silver foil give a modern twist to the cover design.

Print & Finish Foil blocking

Deckle edge

A deckle (or feather) edge is the ragged edge of the paper as it leaves the papermaking machine. Machine-made paper has two deckle edges while handmade paper has four. When not cut away the deckle edge can be used to great decorative effect. Equally the effect can be imitated by tearing the edge of the paper by hand, as the example opposite shows.

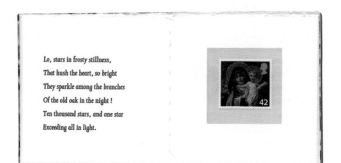

Lo, stars in frosty stillness,
That hush the heart, so bright
They sparkle among the branches
Of the old oak in the night !
Ten thousand stars, and one star
Exceeding all in light.

This spread is taken from *The Wonder Night,* a book of Christmas stamps designed by Irene von Treskow.

The Wonder Night (above and right)

This is a hand-produced, limited-edition book of Christmas stamps that was created by Webb & Webb design studio for Royal Mail. The stamps were designed by Irene von Treskow and depict scenes from 'The Wonder Night'; a poem by Laurence Binyon.

The pages feature a horizontal imitation deckle edge. This was produced by tearing off the edge of the paper and lends a handmade quality to the publication.

Print & Finish Finishing

Client: Royal Mail
Design: Webb & Webb
Technical overview:
Handmade imitation
deckle edge

The Wonder Night

Fore-edge printing

Fore-edge printing uses a special process to print on the cut, outside edges of the book block of a publication. This process finds its origins in gilding, a process that applied gold or silver to the pages of a book to protect them but nowadays is used more commonly to add decorative effects.

This is a gold leaf fore-edge print taken from a publication created by dixonbaxi design studio.

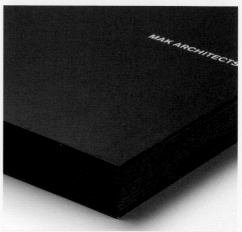

This black, fore-edge print was created by Studio Myerscough for Black Dog Publishing and homogenises the pages with the cover, transforming the book into a seemingly solid object.

White Book (right)

This is the *White Book*, which was produced by SEA Design for paper merchant GF Smith, and contains details of the company's updated identity. A silver fore-edge print reflects light as the reader turns the pages, and complements the silver typography used. The book contains creative photographs of ink as can be seen on its cover.

oth

ion

ression

Book

Elements

le

Client: GF Smith
Design: SEA Design
Technical overview:
Silver fore-edge print
reflects light

Endpapers

Endpapers are the heavy cartridge paper pages that are found at the front and back of a hardback book and join the book block to the hardback binding.

Endpapers can be made into an additional decorative feature of a publication as they often feature designs, motifs or maps, or the use of coloured stock.

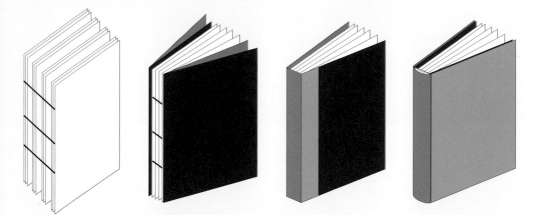

To apply endpapers, the sections of a book block are first collated. Sheets of cartridge paper are then glued on along their folds and one is pressed against the facing edge of the spine and one to the spine on the other side of the book block. Finally, the hard cover is then glued and attached to the endpapers to produce the finished casebound book.

Endpapers add an element of texture to a book as they use a different stock from the rest of the publication.
Left: a bright-coloured stock contrasts with the white of the text block.
Right: screen-printed endpapers secure the text block.

Client: Diesel

Design: Vasava

Technical overview:

Endpapers with a decorative design

"It's not my company, it's my life"

In 1985 Renzo Rosso bought out his business partner, gaining full ownership of the brand that he felt had an astronomical future: Diesel. The result was like striking oil. For 20 years and beyond, Renzo has remained immersed in the company, while pumping his singular vision across the globe.

Fifty

This is *Fifty*; a book created for the Diesel clothing label by Spanish design studio Vasava. The book has endpapers that feature a pattern design that uses the number '50', which is in keeping with the theme of the book's content.

Perforation

Perforation (or perf cutting) is a process that creates a cut-out area in a substrate, which weakens it for detaching.

Perforations are made using perforating blades that can be shaped into a given pattern, so that the cut area of the blade slices through the stock, while the uncut segment (or tie) of the blade does not.

Mailer (above and right)

Pictured right is a mailer outer for a self-promotional piece for design studio George & Vera. As the brochure is perforated it can be mailed without the need to enclose it in a separate envelope. Simple printed instructions tell the user how to access the showcase of George & Vera's work, which is shown inside.

Client: George & Vera
Design: George & Vera
Technical overview:
Brochure/mailer with
perforation

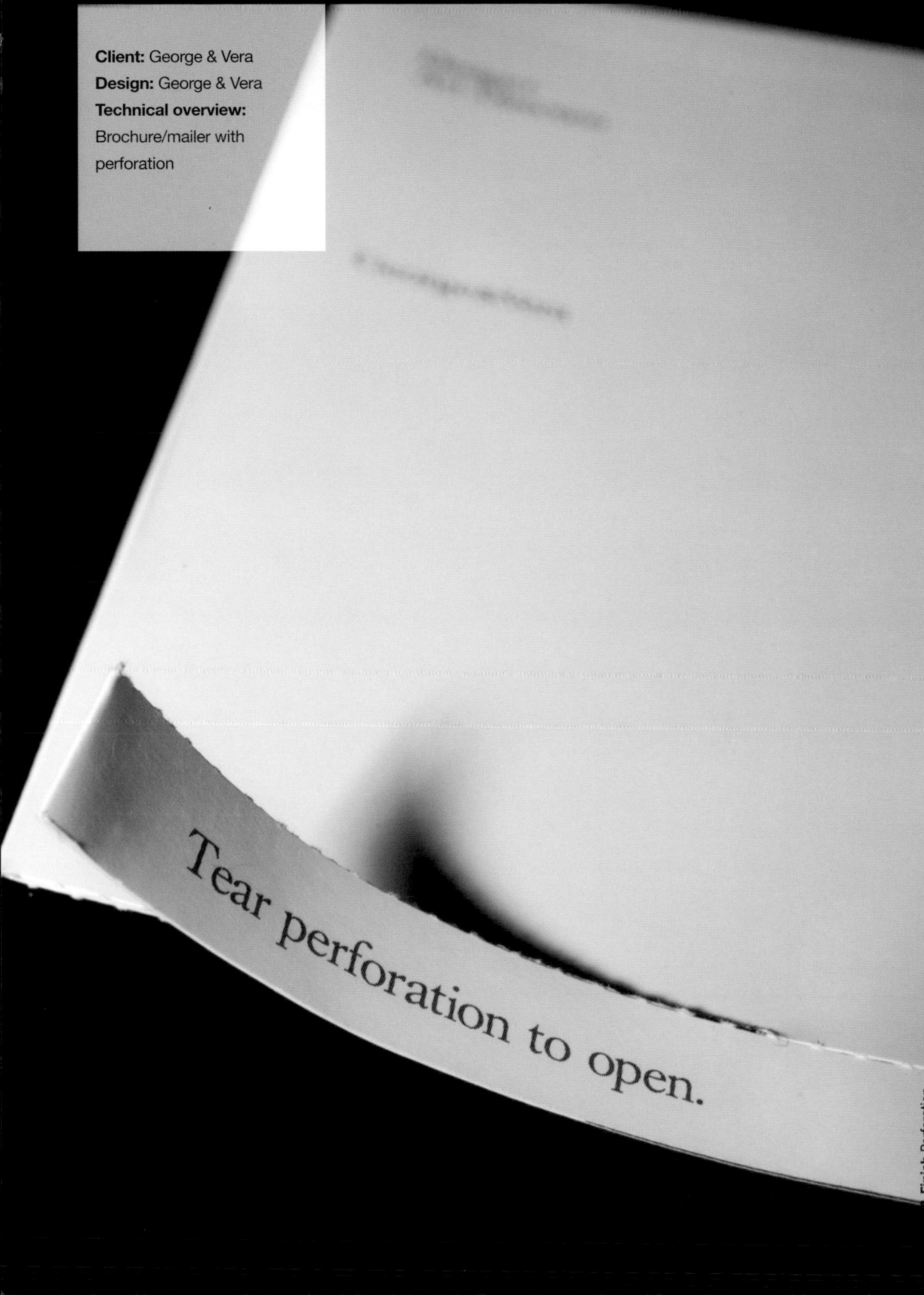

Tear perforation to open.

& Finish Perforation

Client: Persistence Works
Design: Rocca Creative
Technical overview:
Combination of raster and
vector graphics

Open Studios

Friday 25 November 11am-4pm and special evening event with live music and
refreshments from 6pm-9pm.
Saturday 26 November 11am-5pm with copper beating workshops.

More information:
Yorkshire ArtSpace Society
Persistence Works
21 Brown Street
Sheffield
S1 2BS

t/f: 0114 276 1769
e: info@artspace. co.uk
w: www.artspace.org.uk

Production

The production processes used in graphic design and the printing industry, to physically put ink on paper, can be harnessed in many ways to produce creative results. These may include manipulating the colour channels and printing plates, overprinting or reversing out and changing the order in which the process colours print. The impact and creative potential of a design can be enhanced when you control the creative process, rather than letting it control you, as the following pages will show.

This section is printed with metallic (Pantone 8062) and fluorescent orange (Pantone 811) special colours to illustrate the dramatic difference that they can make to a design.

This spread prints with subtle pastel (Pantone 9101) special as a base colour. This special pastel ink also appears on pages 98–99, 102–103, 106–107. The black ink on this page overprints the base colour to remove any ink-trapping issues.

The image on the opposite page knocks out of the base colour, allowing its white areas to contrast with the surrounding colour border. This border is also printed as a graduating blend, from 100% at the bottom of the page, fading to 0% at the top.

Open Studios (left)

This is a poster created by Rocca Creative design studio for the Open Studios event held at Persistence Works, a purpose-built venue for the Yorkshire ArtSpace Society in the UK. The poster features an image of the building that is rendered through a combination of photographic (raster) and illustrated (vector based) graphics to emphasise the link between the building and the visual arts produced inside.

Rasters and vectors
Rasters (photographs) and vectors (illustrations) are the mainstay image formats of printed material today.

This image of a swimmer (shown left) is a raster file that, at this size, looks clear and of photographic quality. However, a limitation of the raster format is that it does not contain sufficient information to produce a clear image when enlarged, as pixelation begins to occur (A). In this context, pixels are also referred to as artefacts.

A raster file can be turned into a vector file for graphic effect. The picture on the opposite page has been enlarged, but as it is a vector file, even a large degree of upsizing produces recognisably sharp lines (B).

However, remember that a poor quality raster image is still an image that does not contain enough information to be reproduced clearly. Rasters are turned into vectors for creative effect, not to solve resolution issues.

A

Enlargement of a raster file produces artefacts or pixelation, whereby image detail and sharpness is lost.

B

As vector graphics are based on drawn paths they remain crisp regardless of the degree of enlargement. This detail is a 350% enlargement of the image.

Channels and plates
Most printed images are produced using a combination of the C, M, Y and K plates of the four-colour printing process.

Understanding the principle of how the four-colour process builds an image allows the designer to treat each colour pass separately, and in doing so obtain better colour adjustment and/or graphic interventions.

The four process inks are applied via separate printing plates in the cyan, magenta, yellow and black sequence in order to build up an image. Notice the difference that the addition of the black plate (K), makes to the image (left) compared to the C+M+Y version below.

C   C+M   C+M+Y   C+M+Y+K

This is the four-colour image, but with a lower amount of black.

This is the four-colour image with a lower level of overall contrast.

This is a lightened image that has been overprinted with a graduated metallic Pantone 811.

These images are printed with fluorescent Pantone 811.

These images use a metallic silver (Pantone 8062) as a base colour.

The colour channels in these images have been mixed to create dramatic effects.

 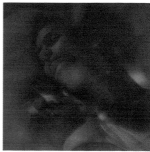

The colour channels in these images have been misregistered and rotated to produce different effects.

Print & Finish Channels and plates

Print order

The order in which each of the CMYK process colours prints has an impact on the resultant printed design.

Understanding this concept requires more than simply knowing the order that the plates print in. Knowledge of the print order is fundamental for understanding overprinting techniques. Logically, only a colour that has already been printed can be 'overprinted' with another colour. In standard printing magenta follows cyan, therefore cyan cannot overprint magenta. Black, however, prints last and therefore can overprint yellow, magenta or cyan. When using varnish you also need to consider whether the special finish will overprint (as the example opposite shows), or knockout.

CMYK

These are the standard process colours in the order that they print; cyan, magenta, yellow and black.

Knockout

A knockout is a gap that is left in the bottom ink layer so that an image printed over it (that overlaps it), appears without colour modification from the ink underneath it. The bottom colour is literally 'knocked-out' of the area where the other colour overlaps. To print a magenta circle on a cyan square, the cyan square must first be printed with a white circle (A). The hole in which the circle will print is slightly smaller than the magenta circle to be printed to avoid ink trapping issues (B). The magenta circle slightly overprints the blue square to avoid any white lines appearing due to misalignment of the two plates (C).

Ink trapping

Ink trapping is the overlapping of areas of coloured text or shapes to compensate for misregistration on the printing press. Ink trapping is required because the halftone dots that make up printed images overlap (because they are of different sizes and at different screen angles); therefore, the colours must also be overlapped to prevent the appearance of white gaps where they are supposed to meet.

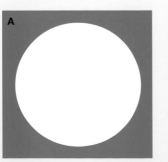

A

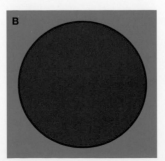

B

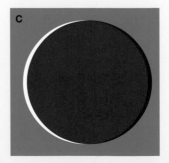

C

Client: Oskar de Kiefte
Design:
Faydherbe / De Vringer
Technical overview:
Special varnish applied after
printing as final pass

40% Auto

40% Auto is a
book/catalogue created
by artist Oskar de Kiefte,
and designed by
Faydherbe / De Vringer.
The design concept is
based on that of a mail-
order catalogue, and the
artist's work is presented
as products that can be
purchased. The title
reflects the fact that 40%
of de Kiefte's projects
involve cars. The book's
cover is printed in black
and red, with a special
shiny varnish that
overprints the red text to
create a subtle two-tone
effect. The red ink
contains metallic silver to
imitate the highly
reflective nature of traffic
signs, which glow when
car headlights hit them.

Print & Finish Print order

Overprinting techniques
Overprinting, surprinting and reversing out can all be used to great creative effect.

An overprint describes the printing of one colour on top of another. A surprint is where a percentage or tone of a colour is used; and a reverse out is where the white (or colour) of the page or substrate is used and the printed colour forms the background or base colour.

CMYK
These are the four process colours; they are usually printed in the CMYK order.

Knockout
The default setting on most software is for colours to knockout so that pure colours are preserved.

Overprint
Colour application can be set to overprint, which allows the colours to interfere with one another.

Additional colours
Additional colours can be printed at any pass during the printing process, although it is worth remembering that a special colour will be printed in the same position on all pages of the section in which it is used. So, for example, if silver prints first, it cannot be set to overprint on another page within the same section.

 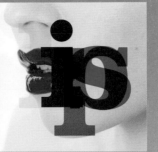 

Above: typography overprinting raster graphics.

Above: layered colour panels overprinting monotone raster images.

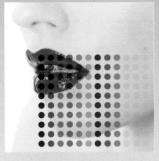  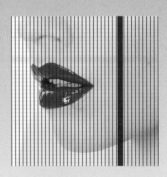

Above: patterns overprinting an image.

Above : black panels of 100% (left), 80% (middle), and 60% (right) graduations, overprinting colour images.

Juice (above)

This is a simple design by Parent design studio for *Juice* magazine. The title of the article is presented in translucent red text that overprints the opening, full-page image. This allows the image to showthrough the type.

Piano Factory (right)

This is a property brochure created by MadeThought design studio for London & Overseas. The brochure incorporates a concertina fold that nestles within the flaps of a hard cover without any form of binding. The brochure's four-colour images have sections of flood black that overprint, which creates a textured and layered effect.

Client: London & Overseas
Design: MadeThought
Technical overview:
Black allowed to overprint
the four-process colours
for creative effect

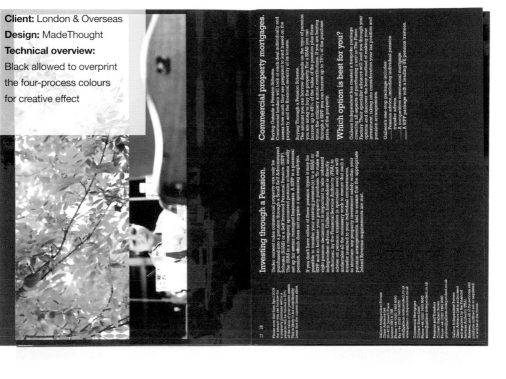

Commercial property mortgages.

Buying Outside a Pension Scheme.
Commercial lenders will both at each deal individually and assess how much they are prepared to lend based on the property and the financial security of its tenants.

Buying Through a Pension Scheme.
The amount you can borrow depends on the type of pension you are using to buy the property. For a SSAS you can borrow up to 50% of the value of the pension plus three times the ordinary annual contributions. If you are buying through a SIPP you can borrow up to 75% of the purchase price of the property.

Which option is best for you?

Galleon Independent has created a bespoke package covering all aspects of purchasing commercial property. From a single specialist advisor, we will take you through your options and discover the best method of making your investment, taking into consideration your tax position and pension arrangements.

Galleon's one-stop package includes:
— Pension advice, including individual pension transfer advice.
— A competitive commercial mortgage.
— A SIPP package with a leading UK pension trustees.

Investing through a Pension.

Under current rules commercial property can only be purchased into a pension through a Small Self-Administered Scheme (SSAS) or a Self Invested Personal Pension (SIPP). The SSAS is a company sponsored pension scheme usually set up for owner-managed businesses. A SIPP is a personal pension, which does not require sponsorship by an employer.

If you don't have either of these pension types it may be possible to transfer your existing pension(s) to a SSAS or SIPP and so facilitate your property purchase. To make the right pension decisions it is important to take unbiased independent advice. Galleon Independent is directly authorised by the Financial Service Authority (FSA) to advise on pension transfers (a specialist area) and will undertake all the necessary work to ensure that such a transfer is sound and commercially appropriate. We can also advise on the most tax-efficient way to structure any property investment safely within your pension arrangements, and to ensure that the appropriate Inland Revenue requirements are met.

Galleon Independent Private
Client Advisors
St James's Place
London SW1A 1NR
Tel +44 (0)20 7499 9000
Fax +44 (0)20 7493 9070
office@galleon-independent.co.uk
www.galleon-independent.co.uk

Commercial Mortgages
Phone +44 (0)20 7499 8000
Fax +44 (0)20 7499 9070
office@galleon-independent.co.uk

Pension and Trustees
Phone +44 (0)20 7499 8000
Fax +44 (0)20 7499 9070
office@galleon-independent.co.uk

Galleon Independent Private Client Advisors Ltd is authorised and regulated by the Financial Services Authority (FSA). However, not all of the services and products mentioned are regulated, or will be in the future.

Buy Your Own 'Strata' Office in Central London.

London & Overseas is now making it possible for you to own your own office in Central London. Buy it for your own occupation or for investment.

A 'strata' office is simply a single floor of an office building. You can now buy a long leasehold office like you would buy a flat. A management company takes care of the fabric of your building and all of the other strata office owners contribute a fair portion of those costs, as with a leasehold block of flats.

In the UK, for more than a hundred years, people have been happy to live in flats on a leasehold basis. Now you can own a long leasehold office.

The concept of owning an office like we own a flat is relatively new in this country. However, in many other countries, buying a leasehold office is very much a normal part of business. Other countries call this buying a strata office.

— The concept of buying a long lease office, a strata office, will be very much tried and tested in ten years.
— The strata concept is a new and growing business in the UK.

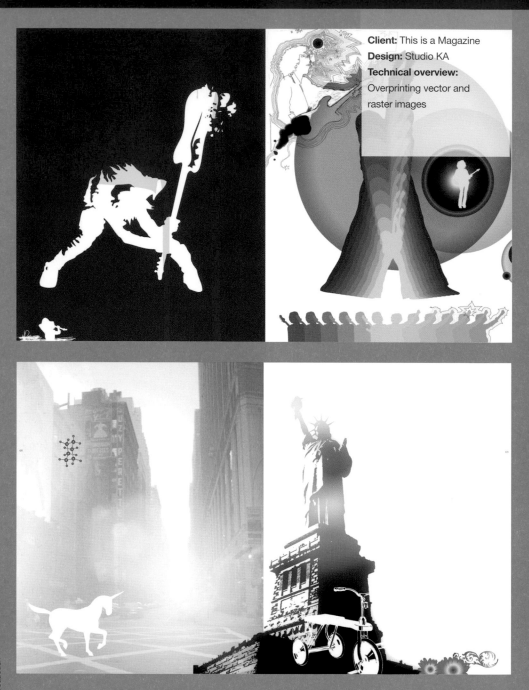

Client: This is a Magazine
Design: Studio KA
Technical overview:
Overprinting vector and
raster images

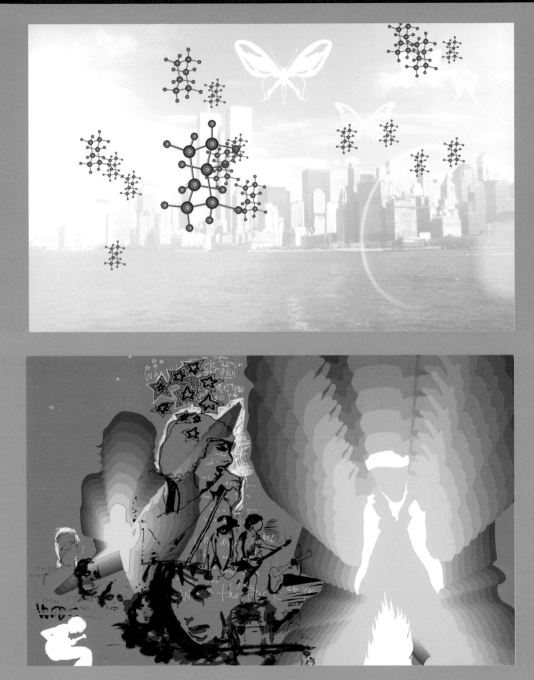

This is a Magazine (above and left)

These are spreads taken from *This is a Magazine*, and were created by Studio KA using vector and raster image elements. The different components of the design overprint; creating a textured graphic tapestry of colour and form.

Print & Finish Overprinting techniques

Halftones
A halftone is an image composed of different-sized dots, which reproduce the continuous tones of a photograph.

The dots, which can be formed from various shapes, can be manipulated in terms of their size, spacing and screen angle, as the examples below illustrate.

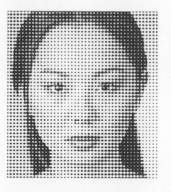

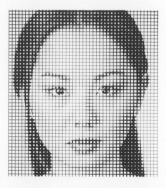
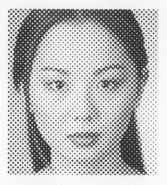

This is the base image.

This image uses enlarged halftone dots.

The use of halftone lines produces a graphic effect.

The halftone lines in this image are at an angle, which provides a hatching effect.

Rather than dots, this halftone image is produced from ellipses.

This images uses halftone squares.

Zembla (right)
These spreads were created by Frost Design for literary magazine *Zembla*. The image elements of the spreads have been rendered with a dot-shaped halftone effect.

Client: Zembla Magazine

Design: Frost Design

Technical overview:

Dot-halftone rendered images

FICTION TWO

zembla magazine [72]   zembla magazine [73]

FICTION TWO

The
Accident
A reconstruction in three parts
By James Flint

[70] zembla magazine   zembla magazine [71]

Tonal images

A tonal image is akin to a black-and-white photograph in which the white tones have been replaced by one of, or a combination of, the other CMY process colours.

Turning the original photograph (far left) into a greyscale image (left), creates a duotone.

This is a basic duotone produced using cyan and black.

In this duotone the cyan flooding has been increased to produce a darker effect.

This is a tritone using cyan and magenta, which produces a warmer effect.

This is a flooded magenta duotone.

This is a duotone produced using yellow, which produces a warm, soft result.

This is a tritone using yellow and red.

This quadtone image produces a greater contrast and shadow depth.

These duotone images use silver and a fluorescent (left and middle) and then a fluorescent and black duotone.

The colour curves on these duotones have been adjusted to give different intensity to the tonal colour.

If the colour values are adjusted far enough a negative looking image can be produced.

Experimentation with the colour curves can produce very graphic results.

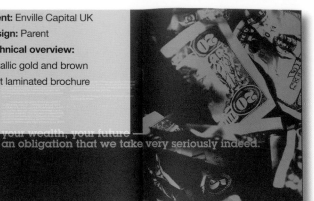

Client: Enville Capital UK

Design: Parent

Technical overview:

Metallic gold and brown
print laminated brochure

your wealth, your future —
an obligation that we take very seriously indeed.

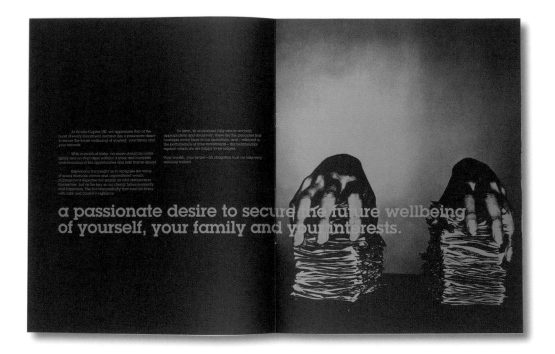

At Enville Capital UK, we appreciate that at the heart of every investment decision lies a passionate desire to secure the future wellbeing of yourself, your family and your interests

With so much at stake, no move should be made lightly and no step taken without a clear and complete understanding of the opportunities and risks that lie ahead.

Experience has taught us to recognize the value of sound financial advice and unparalleled wealth management expertise not simply as vital elements in themselves, but as the key to our clients' future prosperity and happiness. This is a responsibility that must be borne with care and constant vigilance.

To listen, to understand fully and to act both appropriately and decisively: these are the passions that underpin every facet of our operations, and – reflected in the performance of your investments – the benchmarks against which we are happy to be judged.

Your wealth, your future – an obligation that we take very seriously indeed.

a passionate desire to secure the future wellbeing
of yourself, your family and your interests.

Enville Capital UK

This brochure showcases the services of wealth management company Enville
Capital UK. It prints metallic gold and brown, colours that give a warm, refined and
opulent feel. This is enhanced by the spacious layout and spartan use of text
juxtaposed against full-bleed photography. The brochure is laminated to give the
stock additional substance and a more luxurious feel.

Client: Land Securities

Design: NB: Studio

Technical overview:

Highly-saturated, four-colour photographic and duotone images with gradient fade

Land Securities

This is a brochure created by NB: Studio for Land Securities for a series of property developments in London. Highly-saturated, four-colour photographic images are used to convey the 'love shopping' theme (pictured bottom) and these contrast sharply with the duotone images of the property developments. The duotones also feature a gradient fade from top to bottom.

Tints

A tint is a shade of a colour that has been diluted, through the addition of white, in order to create a paler variation of it.

Colour reproduction is usually achieved by screening the three trichromatic process colours; cyan, magenta and yellow, in increments of 10%. This produces 1,330 available tints for the designer to use, and this increases to almost 15,000 when black is included as well. The swatch below shows 10% incremental tints of black and prints on a green stock. This demonstrates that even if using a limited colour palette, the use of non-white stocks can produce colour variation and give the illusion that several colours have been incorporated.

| 10% | 20% | 30% | 40% | 50% | 60% | 70% | 80% | 90% | 100% |

Above: increments of image values from 10% to 100%.

Above: 100% black images over different values of tinted boxes.

Above: a series of duotones using 100% black images with another base colour in increments from 10% to 100%.

Client: one.org
Design: Research Studios
Technical overview:
Tints of black and varied
point sizes produce a
dramatic presentation

ONE

ONE BILLION PEOPLE WATCH THE ACADEMY AWARDS. **ONE** BILLION PEOPLE LIVE IN EXTREME POVERTY. STAND WITH THEM. WEAR THE WHITE BAND TO FIGHT GLOBAL AIDS AND POVERTY.

BONO, GEORGE CLOONEY, SALMA HAYEK, DENNIS HOPPER, AL PACINO, ELLEN DEGENERES, DJIMON HOUNSOU, TOM HANKS, BENICIO DEL TORO, ANTONIO BANDERAS, JACK VALENTI, RICHARD CURTIS AND FRIENDS OF THE GLOBAL FIGHT

ONE THE CAMPAIGN TO MAKE POVERTY HISTORY. **ONE.ORG**

one.org

This poster was created by Research Studios as part of the branding and design campaigns for one.org, the website of a widely publicised campaign to make poverty history and combat AIDS. The poster features text in different tints of black and in different point sizes to give a dramatic presentation to the content.

Print & Finish Tints

Client: The London Institute
Design: Turnbull Grey
Technical overview:
Sewn-side binding for visual
and tactile properties

PARTICLE
FABRICS
2002

Binding

Binding is the collective term for the range of processes that are used to hold together the pages or sections of a publication to form a book, magazine, brochure or other format. The different binding methods available allow a designer to make choices about the functionality of a publication in addition to its visual qualities, permanence and cost. Used creatively, binding can provide a simple means of differentiating a publication and adding a special touch.

Binding choices have a direct influence on the durability of a publication; sewn or burst binding are more durable methods than perfect binding, for example. Consumer magazines have a short shelf life and so saddle stitching or perfect binding is typically used as these methods are cheaper and their durability for the format is of less importance. If a publication needs to lie flat, which is often the case for manuals, wiro or Canadian binding is more appropriate.

Particle Fabrics (left)

This publication was created by Turnbull Grey for higher-education establishment The London Institute. As the publication deals with fabrics, Turnbull Grey chose to use materials that add textural elements to the design; these included a sewn-side binding and French fold pages. These elements also enhance the visual appearance, and perceived quality and durability of the publication.

Wiro, spiral and comb binding
Wiro binding is characterised by a metal spine that passes through specially cut holes in the binding edge of a publication.

The main benefit of this binding method is that it allows the pages of the publication to lie flat, as can be seen in the example opposite. It also leaves the spine uncovered, as can be seen in the illustration below. Care needs to be taken with any images that cross the gutter of the document, where the punch-holes can interfere with the aesthetic.

Wiro binding
Opposed metal teeth 'bite' through holes that are cut in the pages, and meet to bind the pages.

Spiral binding
A metal spiral is fed, from the top to the bottom (or vice versa), through holes that are cut in the pages, to bind the publication. This process is more time consuming, but holds the pages more securely.

Comb binding
This follows the same principle as wiro binding, but uses a plastic comb rather than metal teeth.

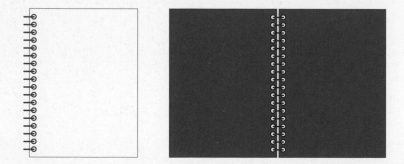

Eurostar (right)
This is a brochure created by HGV Felton for rail company Eurostar. It has five wiro-bound leaves and 12 short, varnished tip-ins, which are used to represent the Solari analogue information display system that is used in airports and rail stations to convey information about flight or train times. The rich, atmospheric black-and-white imagery draws attention to the spine of the publication where the wire binding is used as the hinge in the message system, which invites the reader to interact with it.

Client: Eurostar
Design: HGV Felton
Technical overview:
Wiro binding with tip-ins
to represent information
display system

esprit europe is the leading supplier of timetabled parcel services between central London and central Paris and Brussels. Esprit Europe has introduced a new dimension to the city to city parcels business. Up to 20 Eurostar trains each day offer door to door deliveries in as little as four hours. Alongside the pioneering Euro sameday service, the innovative next day Euro by 9 service completes a unique package of services. Our customers include some of the largest alongside some of the smallest companies in London – they all value the specialist service from Esprit Europe.

BRUSSELS

Canadian binding
Canadian binding takes two forms: Canadian and half-Canadian, although both methods are essentially the same.

Both Canadian and half-Canadian binding utilise a wiro, which is set within a wraparound cover to hold the pages of a publication together. Both methods allow the document to lie flat, and to have a spine to carry titling and volume information.

Full-Canadian bind
A Canadian or full-Canadian bind has a covered spine, as in the illustration shown below left.

Half-Canadian bind
A half-Canadian bind has notches in the cover that expose the spine, as in the illustration shown below right.

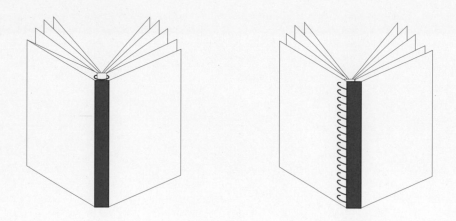

In this example, the text block (A) is Canadian bound to a base of the same size (B). This valley folds into two panels (C), which are large enough to hold it, and a cover spine (D), which allows the publication to be closed. All the folds are indicated in magenta.

C   D   C   B   A

Client: Arts Council England
Design: Untitled
Technical overview:
Canadian binding and die-
cut corners

Necessary Journeys

This publication, which is a record of the physical and metaphorical journeys of a
group of artists,was created by Untitled design studio for the Arts Council England.
The publication uses full-Canadian binding, which consists of a wiro (spiral wire) set
within a wraparound cover that encloses the spine so that the wire is not visible. The
publication has die-cut corners that become progressively shorter to form a tabbing
reference system for the pages.

Self binds
Certain publications can appear to be bound, when in fact the only print finishing process that has been used is folding.

Such publications are described as self binds because the reader manually rebinds the publication after using it by folding it again. Maps and brochures are typical examples of self binds.

This illustration is an example of a publication featuring an accordion fold in which the first two panels (highlighted in magenta) form a cover that the other panels fold into. The first two panels are larger than the others to allow for creep.

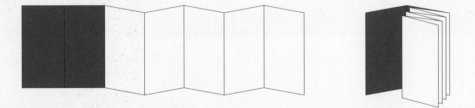

Situations Annual Report (below and right)

This annual report was created by Thirteen design studio on behalf of Situations. Launched in 2003, Situations set out to commission new art within a context of critical debate and discussion. This report summarises the programme's diverse and cumulative impact to date. Instead of a formal binding for this 30-page publication, Thirteen chose to use an accordion fold. One side of the report provides factual information about audience figures, finances and funding while the other side presents the organisation's vision, mission and information about its projects and publications. Printed in two parts and finished by hand, the pages incorporate subtle colour graduations to represent Situation's ability to change fluidly.

Client: Situations

Design: Thirteen

Technical overview:

Accordion fold that contains

all pages

Case binding
Case or edition binding is a durable method often used in the production of hardback books.

Vellum

Vellum is a translucent paper that is sometimes used to protect colour plates in a book. It is available in different patterns or textured effects such as linen.

Buckram

Buckram is a coarse linen or cotton fabric, sized with glue or gum, which is used for covering a hardcover binding.

Headbands and tailbands

Headbands and tailbands are pieces of cloth tape that cover the top and bottom of the spine for both decorative and protective purposes.

Endpapers

Endpapers are the sheets of heavy, cartridge-paper stock that are found at the front and back of a case-bound book, and which join the book block to the binding.

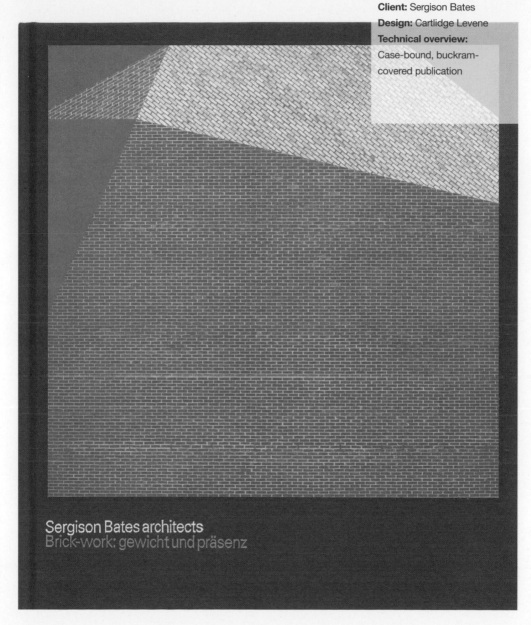

Client: Sergison Bates
Design: Cartlidge Levene
Technical overview:
Case-bound, buckram-
covered publication

Sergison Bates architects
Brick-work: gewicht und präsenz

Brick-work

This is *Brick-work*, a publication created by Cartlidge Levene design studio for Sergison Bates architects. This case-bound book's title is screen-printed into the buckram cloth covering.

Print & Finish Case binding

Perfect binding
Perfect, or unsewn, binding is a method that is commonly used for magazines and paperback books.

To perfect bind a publication, the sections are formed into a block and the binding edge is glued with a flexible adhesive, which holds them together without the use of stitches and also attaches the cover.

The binding edge may sometimes be cut to allow the adhesive to have greater purchase, which is why the method is sometimes called cut-back binding. The fore-edge is then trimmed to give a clean, straight finish. The quality of the adhesive will determine how durable this binding is.

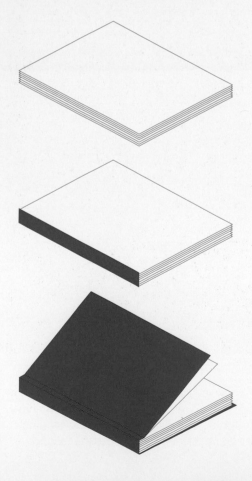

Perfect-binding process
The signatures are collated and formed into a book block. The spines are cut away or notched and adhesive is applied. A cover is then attached and folded around the book block. Finally, the fore-edge is trimmed. Notice that the spine edge is pinched. In essence, the pinch acts as the fulcrum for page turning that gives the gutter space and prevents weakening the spine.

Section sewing
The sections of the book block can be thread sewn prior to being bound to give added strength, but this process takes longer and is consequently more expensive.

Thread sealing
This process combines perfect binding and section sewing but there is no thread running between the sections.

Side sewing
This method uses a thread that goes from the front to the back of the text block. It produces an extremely strong binding and therefore, unsurprisingly, it is often used in children's books.

Client: RSA
Design: Untitled
Technical overview:
Perfect-bound brochure with
emboss, deboss and die cut to
enhance black-on-black effect

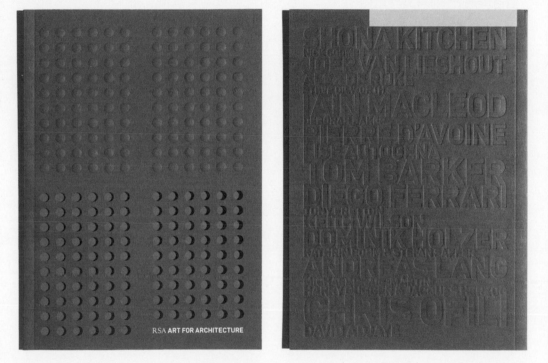

RSA **ART FOR ARCHITECTURE**

RSA (above)

This is the Art For Architecture brochure, which was produced for the Royal Society of Architecture by Untitled design studio. The front cover features a black stock that combines an embossed circle design with a die cut, which creates a black-on-black effect that also adds texture to the piece. The back cover features the artists whose work is contained in the brochure as a deboss.

Print & Finish Perfect binding

Alternative bindings
Unusual techniques or materials can supply a range of creative binding effects.

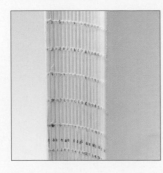

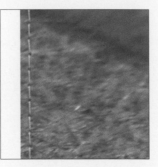

Open bind
An open bind has visible stitching; this example is by Tank design studio for *Mind* magazine.

Bellyband
This publication, created by MadeThought design studio, is enhanced and contained by a bellyband.

Singer stitch
Stitch binding can add a decorative touch as thread is available in many weights and colours, and indeed, can be sewn in a variety of patterns.

Z-binds
This z-bind publication was created by MadeThought design studio. Z-binding clearly separates a publication into two parts.

Elastic bands
Elastic bands provide a simple way of holding loose-leaf sheets together with a rigid cover stock.

Clips and bolts
Clips and bolts and other hardware can be used for binding purposes; as this example by Studio Myerscough design studio shows.

Client: Land Securities
Design: NB: Studio
Technical overview:
Bellyband for closure and
visual element

Land Securities

This is a brochure called *Capital Commitment*, which was created by NB: Studio
for property development firm Land Securities. The brochure features a printed
and foil-blocked bellyband that holds its pages closed in addition to providing
a distinctive visual element. The bellyband is marked 'Life*Style*', a slogan that
incorporates the client's initials and alludes to the suggestion that the 'right'
living space can complement your lifestyle.

Print & Finish Alternative bindings

Client: The Conran Shop
Design: Studio Myerscough
Technical overview:
Elastic-band binding

Juxtapose With You

This brochure was created for furnishing retailer
The Conran Shop by Studio Myerscough. It comprises
a series of juxtaposing loose-leaf pages that are held
together with an elastic band. This binding allows
the reader to remove pages and reassemble the
publication in any way they wish. The spreads pictured
opposite demonstrate this juxtaposition and underline
how the format of the piece mirrors the title of the
collection: 'Juxtapose with You'.

Client: The Mill
Design: MadeThought
Technical overview:
Screen-printed jewel box
gives depth and texture

The resolve of a final product often draws together several of the techniques that are discussed in earlier chapters of this book. Many printed items feature a range of creative printing and finishing processes, which ultimately form the final product.

In previous chapters we have looked at the different areas of print and finishing individually. Most pieces of work, however, combine different elements and techniques of both areas. An understanding of the potential of printing and finishing techniques enables a designer to add value to a design through the creative execution of a brief that may result in an enviable finish. This may translate into a direct benefit for the client as their products and communications become more distinctive than their competitors, and ultimately more exciting to the end user.

The satisfaction and interest generated by creative printing and finishing techniques never ceases to astound. People have an instinctive relationship between what they see and what they touch, and the feel of an interesting stock or the way a foil might catch the light possesses a certain magic, one that a designer can control and use to their advantage.

The Mill (left)

This packaging for a DVD showreel was created by MadeThought design studio for The Mill, a London-based post-production film company. The jewel box outer has been screen printed on both the front and back to give an element of depth to the design while also adding a textural quality to the product. The screen-printing process gives a flat, even, vibrant colour and with a great deal of fine detail, as can be seen in the grid pattern on the reverse, which lends a unique identity to an otherwise bland, standard packaging item.

Texture

Texture can be given to a publication in several ways; these include substrate choice, printing process and the finishing techniques used.

Texture adds a tactile quality to a piece of printed matter and, if used effectively, can make for distinctive graphic executions.

eugène van veldhoven

Dunne Bierkade 29
2512 BD Den Haag / The Hague
The Netherlands

T / F: + 31 (0)70 3655237
eugene@dutchtextiledesign.com
www.dutchtextiledesign.com

eugène van veldhoven

www.dutchtextiledesign.com

eugène van veldhoven

Dunne Bierkade 29
2512 BD Den Haag / The Hague
The Netherlands

T / F: + 31 (0)70 3655237
eugene@dutchtextiledesign.com
www.dutchtextiledesign.com

eugène van veldhoven

www.dutchtextiledesign.com

Eugène van Veldhoven (above and right)

This identity was created by Faydherbe / De Vringer for fabric designer Eugène van Veldhoven. The design concept reflects the occupation of the client, who creates new coatings and fabrics for the fashion and car industries. Insider, a typeface created by Dutch font studio Character Font Foundry, was used for the text, and the logo was hot-foil blocked and embossed on to a coated metallic paper, which gave it a fabric-like texture. Contact details were printed in a metallic ink and the cards were printed with different varnishes and embosses to create a 'wardrobe' of effects.

Client: Eugène van Veldhoven
Design:
Faydherbe / De Vringer
Technical overview:
Foil block and emboss on to
coated metallic paper
produces fabric texture

Client: Circle Press

Design: Thomas Manss & Company

Technical overview:
Embossed cover and pop-up section add texture

Cathy Courtney The Looking Book

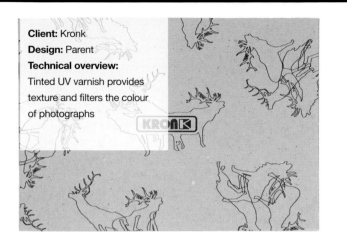

Client: Kronk
Design: Parent
Technical overview:
Tinted UV varnish provides texture and filters the colour of photographs

Look book
A look book is typically a collection of images relating to upcoming trends in the fashion industry. However, the concept has now been widened to encompass any collection of reference images or catalogue about a given subject.

The Looking Book (left)

The Looking Book was created by Thomas Manss & Company for the 13th anniversary of Circle Press, a company that specialises in publishing unique, imaginative limited-edition books using a range of print processes and finishes. The embossed cover (top), and pop-up section in the centre of the book (bottom right), are original pieces by Circle Press founder and artist Ron King. The other images are taken from *Turn Over Darling*, a series of six drawings in wire by Ron King.

Kronk Look Book (above)

This look book was created for UK fashion label Kronk by Parent design studio. The brochure cover features a metallic pink logo that is foil blocked into greyboard as part of the publication's 'hyper natural' theme. The spreads are printed five colour with a tinted UV varnish that gives a textured finish and filters the natural colours of the photography.

Print & Finish Texture

Added value

Printing and finishing techniques provide both the designer and the client with the opportunity to add value to a print publication. While the use of such techniques will undoubtedly add to the cost of a print job they can help the piece communicate effectively and in more dimensions. For example, adding a spot varnish to a cover design will give a publication a tactile element that may translate into a higher perceived quality. The reader may associate this higher quality with the product or organisation the publication is from.

Oliver Spencer (right)

This brochure was created by George & Vera design studio for the Spring/Summer 2006 collection of London-based menswear designer Oliver Spencer. The brochure's clean and simple page layout is contained within a four-panel wrap cover to enhance the quality feel of the publication. The brochure is printed on a luxurious uncoated paper stock, and again this alludes to the quality of both the publication and, by association, the clothing line.

Print & Finish Resolve

Client: Oliver Spencer
Design: George & Vera
Technical overview:
Four-panel wrap cover and
luxurious uncoated stock

Client: VH1
Design: dixonbaxi
Technical overview:
Fore-edge printing and
unusual die cut creates
a designed 'object'

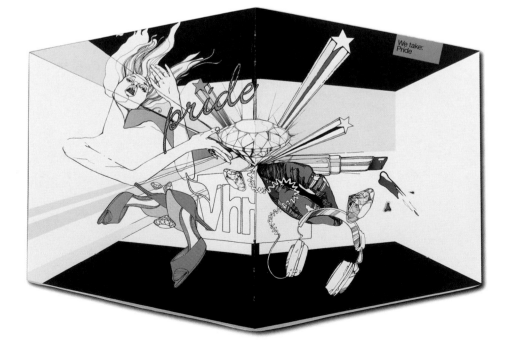

VH1

This publication, containing the corporate guidelines for cable TV channel VH1, was created by dixonbaxi design studio. dixonbaxi used the theme of TV idents, which are by nature varied and fleeting, to direct the content. The result is an eclectic array of text and images that is intended to convey a sense that the guidelines are neither prescriptive or restrictive.

The publication has gold fore-edge printing and is die cut in the shape of the channel's logo, creating a designed 'object', rather than just a printed book. The use of fore-edge printing on a publication about an instantaneous medium makes an interesting subversion of the intended longevity the process suggests.

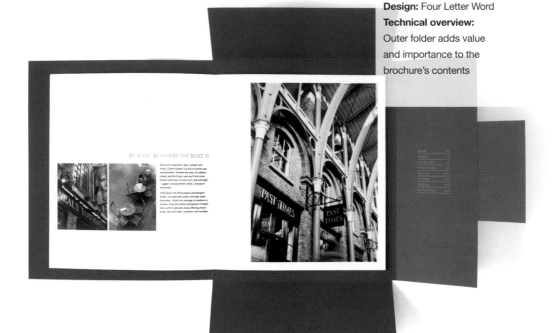

Client: E A Shaw
Design: Four Letter Word
Technical overview:
Outer folder adds value
and importance to the
brochure's contents

E A Shaw (above)

This promotional brochure for E A Shaw's Ingram House property development in London was created by Four Letter Word design studio. The way the folder contains the inner brochure conveys a sense of value and lends an importance to its contents, in addition to serving as a protective outer. As a property brochure, it will inevitably be well thumbed, so providing extra protection through the outer is a practical idea.

Wedgwood (right)

This presentation box, created by Studio Myerscough design studio for fine-china producer Wedgwood, lends a modern touch to a long-standing and traditional brand.

The box is covered with paper and presents a collage design that contains a range of visual elements composed from archival and scanned images and graphic elements, which are combined with an intricate foil pattern. The silver foil maintains the company's classic image as it reflects the ornate moulded designs that embellish Wedgwood's china.

This design concept cleverly revisits traditional values to produce a sense of playful irreverence to an established and historic brand.

Client: Wedgwood
Design: Studio Myerscough
Technical overview:
Ornate foil design combined
with graphics to produce a
modern presentation

Archive Collection

WEDGWOOD

OF BARLASTON

Print & Finish Added value

Glossary

Printing and finishing processes can be employed to add creative value to a design, as the examples showcased in this volume demonstrate. Understanding the terminology that is used to describe and define these processes enables easier communication of aims and intentions between designers, clients and the print industry.

Many of these terms are collected in the following glossary for quick reference. While it is not possible to be exhaustive we have provided the most commonly used terms. An appreciation and knowledge of these will facilitate a better understanding and articulation of the subject. A series of mini guides within the glossary puts many of these terms in context, and serves as a valuable reference section.

Accordion or concertina fold
Two or more parallel folds that go in opposite directions and open out like an accordion.

Bellyband
A printed band that wraps around the belly of a publication; typically used on magazines.

Bible paper
A thin, lightweight, long-life, opaque paper grade typically made from 25% cotton and linen rags or flax with chemical wood pulp, named after its most common usage.

Binding
Any of several processes for holding together the pages or sections of a publication to form a book, magazine, brochure or some other format using stitches, wire, glue or other media.

Binding screws
Used with the Purdue hard cover binding method to secure a front and back cover to the pages.

Bitmap or raster
Any graphic image that is composed of picture elements (pixels), commonly used to reproduce detailed tonal images.

Bouncer
A registration problem that occurs due to the use of the black process colour. It can be resolved by underprinting the other process colours.

Channel
One layer of colour information in an image. A RGB image has three channels, a CMYK image has four and a black-and-white image has just one.

CMYK
Cyan, magenta, yellow and black, the subtractive primaries and four process colours.

Colour fall
The pages of a publication, as depicted in the imposition plan, which will receive a special colour or varnish, or are to be printed on a different stock.

Concertina fold
See Accordion fold.

Deboss
As emboss, but recessed into the substrate.

Die cut
Special shapes cut in a substrate by a steel die.

Duotone
A tonal image that is produced using two colours.

Duplexing
Lamination of two stocks with different properties such as colour.

Dust jacket
A loose cover to protect the boards of an edition bound book.

Emboss
A design stamped with or without ink or foil into a substrate giving a raised surface.

Flock
A speciality stock produced by coating a sheet with size and sprinkling it with a dyed flock powder (made from woollen refuse or vegetable fibre dust), to produce a raised pattern.

Fluorescent colour
A vibrant special colour that cannot be reproduced by combining the process colours.

Foil, heat or hot stamp
Foil pressed on to a substrate using heat and pressure. Also known as block print or foil emboss.

Fore-edge printing
A special printing process for the fore-edge of a publication's pages. Gilding is a form of fore-edge printing.

French fold
A sheet of paper that is only printed on one side and folded with two right-angle folds to form a four-page, uncut section. The section is sewn through the fold while the top edges remain folded and untrimmed.

Gatefold
A type of fold in which the left and right edges fold inwards with parallel folds and meet in the middle of the page without overlapping.

Gradient
A graduation of increasing or decreasing colour(s) applied to an image.

Greyscale
An image that contains shades of grey as well as black and white.

Halftone
The simulation of a continuous tone produced by a pattern of dots.

Imposition
The arrangement of pages in the sequence and position they will appear when printed before being cut, folded and trimmed.

Ink trapping
Overlapping of coloured text or shapes to account for printing misregistration and to prevent the appearance of white gaps.

JPEG (Joint Photographic Experts Group)

A file format for storing photographic images. A JPEG file contains 24-bit colour information (i.e. 6.7 million colours), using compression to discard image information. It is suitable for images with complex pixel gradations but not for flat colour.

Knockout

A gap left in the bottom ink layer so that an overprinted image will appear without colour modification from the ink underneath.

Lacquer

A coating applied to a printed work to provide a high-gloss finish.

Laminate

A stock made by bonding two or more layers together. Typically used to provide a thick cover stock comprising a cheap liner with a printable outer.
Also see Duplexing.

Levels

The amount of colour present within a channel.

Metallic ink

A special printing ink that gives a gold, silver, bronze or copper effect.

Offset lithography

A printing technique in which the ink is transferred from a printing plate to a blanket cylinder and then on to the stock on which it is to be printed. Also called lithography.

Overprint

One element printed over another within a design. Typically, a darker colour will overprint a lighter colour.

Perforation

A series of cuts or holes cut impressed in to a substrate with a die to weaken it for tearing.

Process colours

See CMYK.

Raster

See Bitmap.

Reverse out

The removal of part of a flood colour in order to leave white space.

RGB

Red, green and blue, the additive primary colours.

Screen printing

A low-volume printing method where ink is passed through a screen, which carries a design, on to a substrate.

Silk-screen printing

See Screen printing.

Special colour

A printing ink specially mixed to give a specific colour, including metallic or fluorescent inks.

Spot colour

See Special colour.

Spot varnish

A varnish applied to a specific area of a printed piece.

Stock

The paper to be printed upon.

Substrate

The material or surface to be printed upon.

Surprint

Two elements that are printed on top of one another and are tints of the same colour.

Throw-up

Stock that is folded and bound into a publication in such a way that it can be opened out to a much larger dimension than the publication that contains it.

TIFF (Tagged Image File Format)

A file format for storing halftones and photographic images.

Tint

A colour shade that is predominantly white.

Tip-in

An insert attached to a publication by gluing along the binding edge.

Tonal images

Images produced using black and another colour.

UV coating

Coating applied to a printed substrate that is bonded and cured with ultraviolet light.

Varnish

A clear or tinted liquid shellac or plastic coating put on a printed piece to add a glossy, stain or dull finish, applied like a final ink layer after a piece is printed.

Vellum

A thin sheet of specially prepared calfskin, lambskin, or kidskin leather used as a book-binding material.

Z-bind

A z-shaped cover that is used to join to separate publications, or two parts of the same publication.

Client: Yi-Ban
Design: Four Letter Word
Technical overview:
Die cuts and concertina fold
create landscape logo

Yi-Ban

This is a menu that was created as part of a corporate identity created by Four
Letter Word for Chinese restaurant Yi-Ban in London's Docklands. Four Letter Word
developed a contemporary marque, featuring a stylised landscape within a circle
that is used on Yi-Ban's signage, menus and packaging. Several die cuts in the menu
allow the marque to be physically constructed by its different panels through use of
a concertina fold.

Different electronic file formats have different strengths and weaknesses, and some file formats are more suited to specific tasks than others. For printing purposes, a TIFF (Tagged Image File Format) file, supplied at a minimum resolution of 300 DPI (dots per inch) is considered optimum for reproduction. A JPEG (Joint Photographic Experts Group) file that has been sufficiently compressed can produce comparable results from a smaller file size. Artwork for foil stamps and spot varnishes should be supplied as a vector file such as an EPS (Encapsulated PostScript). Cutting devices, such as the machines that make vinyl transfers, also require artwork in vector format. Generally, EPS files are used for line work and logos as file sizes are small and the images can be enlarged to any size, TIFF files are used for images that will be printed, and JPEG files are used for screen images.

Bitmap

A bitmap (or raster) is a graphic image that is composed of picture elements (pixels). A bitmap is commonly used to reproduce detailed, tonal images such as photographs. This bitmap (left) has been turned into a black-and-white image by reducing the threshold control to 50%. The image is further changed with a diffusion dither (centre), and then a halftone is applied (right), which has bold graphic lines.

Greyscale

A greyscale image is one that contains shades of grey as well as black and white as shown (left). The tones of this greyscale TIFF image can easily be altered in publishing programmes to produce different effects. Here, the black percentage is first reduced (centre), and then inverted (right).

TIFF (Tagged Image File Format)

A TIFF is a flexible method for storing halftones and photographic images. TIFF files are preferred for print production because they use lossless compression, which means that no information is lost and the original quality of the image is retained. The TIFF above (left) has been first turned into a halftone (centre), and then contrast adjusted (right).

EPS (Encapsulated PostScript)

EPS is a picture file format for storing vector or object-based artwork and bitmaps. EPS files can be resized, distorted and colour separated, but no content alteration can usually be made. The pair of images above left are vectors that, even with a high level of enlargement, still have smooth edges. The pair of images above right are produced from raster files (such as a JPEG) and have lost detail and smoothness as they have been enlarged.

JPEG (Joint Photographic Experts Group)

A JPEG file is used for storing photographic images by using compression to discard information, and so produce a smaller file size. This loss of information results in a reduction of image quality. Lightly compressed JPEG files can save a lot of space with little quality loss. This JPEG image (left) has similar quality to a TIFF, but further compression to produce a smaller file size sees quality reduce (centre) and the images begin to show pixelation or artefacts (right).

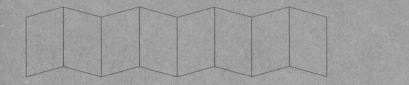

Accordion / Concertina Two or more parallel folds that go in opposite directions and open out like an accordion.

Roll fold Two or more parallel folds that go in the same direction so that the panels fold in on themselves and nest within each other.

Front / back accordion fold With three parallel folds, the two-panel outer wings fold into and out of the centre. The double centre panel serves as the cover.

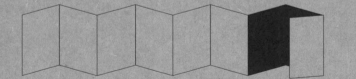

Mock book fold Essentially an accordion fold where the penultimate two panels form a cover that encases the other panels to create a 'book'.

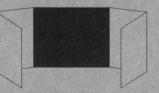
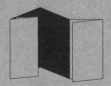

Front / back gatefold An extra double panel that folds inside the front and/or back panel. This fold is often seen on high-quality paperback novels.

Back / front folder Wings either side of the central panel have a double parallel fold so that they can wraparound and cover both sides of the central panel.

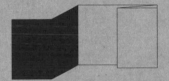

Half cover from behind An accordion fold where the penultimate panel forms a back cover that the other panels fold into to create a book, but the half-size end panel folds around the book from behind to cover the front together with the half-size first panel.

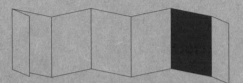

Duelling z-fold The z-fold wings fold into the centre panel and meet in the middle. This fold may be used for promotion brochures or other marketing material.

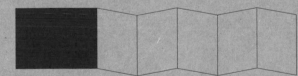

Harmonica self-cover folder An accordion fold where the first two panels form a cover that encases the other panels. The first two panels need to be larger than the others to allow for creep.

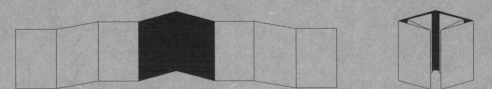

Double gatefold This gatefold has three panels that fold in towards the centre of the publication.

Saddle stitching is a binding method that fastens the loose pages of a publication with wire stitches through the central fold.

Side stitching uses wire stitches to secure pages through the entire thickness of the text block to give additional strength. It is also used to bind several sections together, and can be further bound or covered with tape.

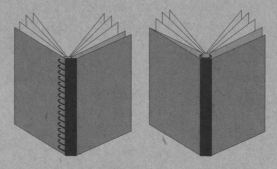

Wiro binding uses a preformed metal gripper that passes through a series of holes punched in the pages.
Comb binding works in the same way, but uses a plastic gripper.
Spiral binding works in a similar way, but the gripper is threaded through the holes and is more durable. All three binding methods allow the open pages of the publication to lie flat.

Canadian binding uses a wiro with a wraparound cover, which combines the benefits of spiral binding (the pages lie flat) with the professional look of perfect binding. With this binding method the spine appears flat, so it is suitable for documents that need to be shelf stored. A Canadian bind (right) has a full covered spine while a half-Canadian bind (left) has a partially exposed spine.

Z-binding uses a z-shaped cover to join two separate publications, or two parts of the same publication. Z-binds offer a convenient solution to the problem of grouping information into distinct sections of a publication. The usual z-bind method is to have two perfect-bound volumes joined by a single cover.

A **bellyband** is a printed band that wraps around and secures the pages of a publication. Bellybands can be produced in a variety of sizes and are typically used with consumer magazines.

Perfect binding is perhaps the most popular method used for producing paperback books. The book's signatures are held together and their spines are ground away to create a rough surface upon which a flexible adhesive is applied to form a spine. A cover board is then attached to the adhesive and the fore-edge is trimmed flat or perfect. For additional strength the sections can be thread sewn or burst bound.

Print & Finish Binding guide

Case-bound book construction

Selecting a suitable book binding method will be a decision that is determined by a range of factors, including the quality, durability, visual impact and cost of the job. A well-finished book adds value to its content and makes it an object that can endure for many years.

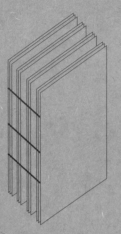   

1. Case binding starts with the collection of the publication's sections to form a book block.

2. Endpapers are then applied to the front and back of the book block.

3. A strip of crash, a starched web of fabric, which is used to connect the book block to the cover, is glued on.

4. Head- and tailbands are glued to the top and bottom of the book block spine and the case is applied.

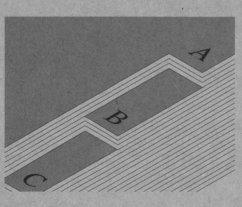

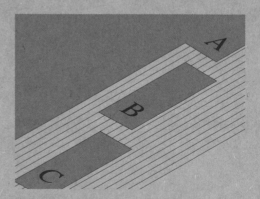

Index cutting

Index cutting is a process whereby a thumb index notch is cut out of the book block to divide different sections or chapters of a publication. This is commonly found on dictionaries and other reference publications.

Tab cutting

A cheaper alternative to index cutting, tab cutting uses single pages to serve as the indicator or reference pages, which are identified by projecting tabs.

Quarter-bound and half-bound books, and jackets

Quarter binding is a method that uses two materials of different qualities for the case, with the better-quality material (such as leather) covering the spine. A half-bound book also sports additional protective corner triangles using the higher-quality material. Ultimately, most hard back editions are finished with an accompanying dust jacket, a loose cover, that protects the boards of the book.

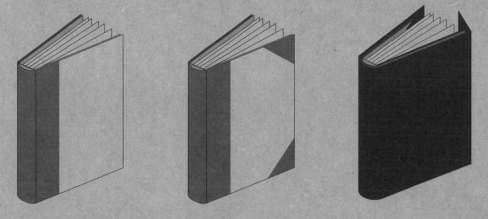

Dust-jacket variations

A standard dust jacket is a loose sheet, usually with flaps of a minimum of 75mm, which is held in place between the endpapers of a case-bound book, or the cover and the text block of a perfect-bound book. A French-fold dust jacket (illustrated below) uses an oversize sheet, which is folded top and bottom, adding bulk and strength, and helping to protect the delicate edges of the paper.

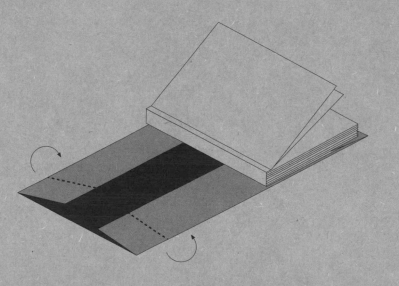

Conclusion

This book explains the basic design principles and methodologies used for printing and print finishing. A thorough understanding of printing processes and finishing techniques will equip the designer with the ability to harness the creative potential of these processes, and add creative elements to a design in order to increase its impact and functionality.

Printing methods and print-finishing techniques create the physical product at the end of the design process. Used in conjunction with thoughtful layout, considered typographic treatments and ingenious image and colour usage, appropriate printing and print finishing not only allows the other design elements to shine, but can also provide added elements of differentiation to distinguish it from other work. We hope that this book proves to be a useful reference when considering how print and print finishing techniques can be integrated and manipulated and serve to enhance a design.

This book should be thought of as a starting point for their exploration. The adventurous use of these techniques requires experimentation, considered thought and inevitably the odd mistake, but armed with the examples and contributions collected together in this volume, a clearer understanding of how each process works can be obtained.

Pierre Cardin (right)

This is a press book created by George & Vera design studio for the spring/summer 2006 product launch of fashion designer Pierre Cardin. The book uses luxurious white space around the images to keep the pages simple, and a vertically-orientated layout, chosen for the typography, adds an interesting visual element. The format includes a four-panel gatefold cover that shows formal wear, within which the main casual wear section is bound to the leading edge.

Client: Pierre Cardin
Design: George & Vera
Technical overview:
Paper section bound to
four-panel gatefold cover

SPRING+ SUMMER KEY LOOKS 2006

Acknowledgements

We would like to thank everyone who supported us during this project including the many art directors, designers and creatives who showed great generosity in allowing us to reproduce their work. Special thanks to everyone who hunted for, collated, compiled and rediscovered some of the fascinating work contained in this book. Thanks to Xavier Young for his patience, determination and skill in photographing the work this volume contains, and a final thank you to Caroline Walmsley, Renée Last, Brian Morris and all the staff at AVA Publishing who never tired of our requests, enquiries and questions, and supported us throughout.

Print & Finish Acknowledgements

Separations (right)

These are proofs of each of the four colour separations. Proofs are used so that the printer and designer can check that the colour reproduction of the printing process is accurate. The proofs contain various graphic devices through which the effectiveness of the printing process can be assessed, such as registration crosshairs, crop marks, colour intensity panels and colour gradient panels. Once approved, the proof will be the measure against which the printed stock will be compared before being accepted.

Project3 28/5/06 5:03 pm Page 1   (Cyan plate)   Project3 28/5/06 5:03 pm Page 1   (Magenta plate)

Project3 28/5/06 5:03 pm Page 1   (Yellow plate)   Project3 28/5/06 5:03 pm Page 1   (Black plate)

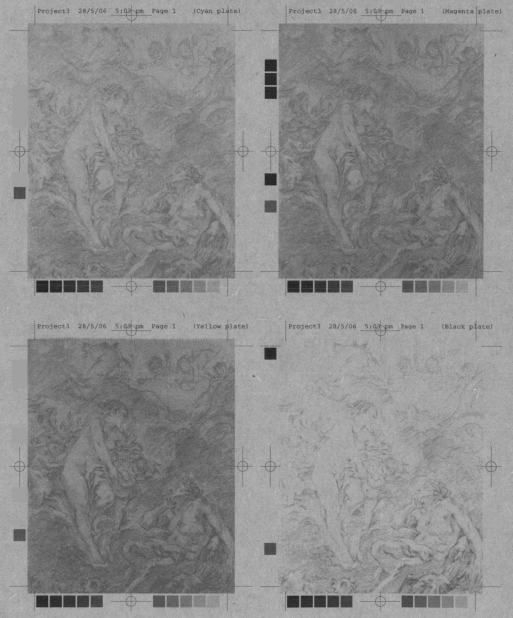